ESSENTIAL KNOTS

Conceived and produced by Weldon Owen
Deepdene Lodge, Deepdene Avenue
Dorking, Surrey, RH5 4AT
Copyright © 2010 Weldon Owen Pty Ltd
First edition: first printing 2010, second printing 2012, third printing 2015, fourth printing 2017, fifth printing 2019, sixth printing 2022
Published in the United States by Skipstone, an imprint of The Mountaineers Books.
www.skipstonebooks.org

WELDON OWEN PTY LTD
Chief Executive Officer Sheena Coupe
Creative Director Sue Burk

Senior Vice President, International Sales Stuart Laurence
Sales Manager: United States Ellen Towell
Vice President, Sales: Asia and Latin America Dawn L. Owen
Administration Manager, International Sales Kristine Ravn
Production Director Todd Rechner
Production Controller Lisa Conway
Production Coordinator Mike Crowton
Production Assistant Nathan Grice

Concept Design Arthur Brown/Cooling Brown
Senior Editor Barbara Sheppard
Editor Shan Wolody
Designers Kristin Mack Alnaes, Christina McInerney
Editorial Assistant Natalie Ryan

Photography Joe Filshie
Photographic styling Georgina Dolling
Photographic retouching Steve Crozier
Hand models Mike Crowton, Jasmine Parker
Index Jo Rudd

Cataloging-in-Publication (CIP) data for this title is on file with the Library of Congress.

ISBN 978-1-59485-485-9

Printed by Toppan Leefung Printing Limited
Manufactured in China

10 9 8 7 6

The paper used in the manufacture of this book is sourced from wood grown in sustainable forests.
It complies with the Environmental Management System Standard ISO 14001:2004

A WELDON OWEN PRODUCTION

This book includes a length of cord for knot-tying practice *only*. It is not intended for games, practical use, or any other applications. The publisher, producer, and authors are not responsible for any adverse consequences resulting directly or indirectly from information contained herein.

LIVE LIFE. MAKE RIPPLES.

CAMPING · CLIMBING · FISHING · SAILING · SCOUTING

ESSENTIAL

KNOTS

The step-by-step guide to tying the *perfect* knot for every situation

NEVILLE OLLIFFE
MADELEINE ROWLES-OLLIFFE

SKIPSTONE

CONTENTS

Introduction 6
Types of cordage 8
Tools 10
Whipping 12
Coiling rope 14

STOPPERS 16
Overhand knot 17
    Multiple overhand 17
    Slipped overhand 18
Figure-of-eight knot 19

BINDINGS 20
Surgeon's knot: binding 21
Reef knot 22
    Granny knot 23
Pole lashing 24
Bag knot 26
    Slipped bag knot 27
Constrictor knot 28
    Slipped constrictor knot 29
Bottle sling 30
Transom knot 32

LOOPS 33
Figure-of-eight loop 34
Surgeon's loop 35
Bowline 36
    Double bowline 37
    Water bowline 38
    Bowline: alternate 39
Bowline on the bight 40
Angler's loop 42
Alpine butterfly knot 44
Blood loop dropper knot 46
Arbor knot 48
Spanish bowline 50
Jury mast knot 52

BENDS.. 54
Figure-of-eight bend............................. 55
Fisherman's knot................................... 56
    Double fisherman's knot 57
    Blood knot 57
Surgeon's knot: bend........................... 58
Carrick bend.. 59
Ashley's bend.. 60
Sheet bend.. 62
    Double sheet bend 63
One-way sheet bend............................ 64
Rigger's bend.. 65

HITCHES... 67
Cow hitch.. 68
    Pedigree cow hitch...................... 69
    Cow hitch and toggle.................. 69
Pile hitch... 70
    Double pile hitch......................... 71
Clove hitch.. 72
    Clove hitch: alternate.................. 73
Marlinspike hitch 74
Barrel hitch... 75
Anchor bend.. 76
    Round turn & two half hitches..... 77
Prusik knot.. 78
Buntline hitch....................................... 79
Highwayman's hitch............................. 80
Timber hitch... 82
    Killick hitch 82
Rolling hitch.. 83
    Tautline hitch.............................. 84
Topsail halyard bend 85
Palomar knot... 86
Snelling a hook..................................... 88
Trucker's hitch...................................... 90

LASHINGS.. 92
Square lashing....................................... 93
Diagonal lashing 95
Sheer lashing... 97
Tripod lashing 99

SPLICES.. 101
Eye splice.. 102
Short splice 104

TRICKS.. 106
Impossible knot.................................... 107
Handcuffs puzzle 108
Ring drop.. 109
Not a knot 110

DECORATIVE.. 111
Monkey's fist.. 112
Kringle mat 114
Ocean mat 116
Knife lanyard knot 118
    Chinese button 120
Double Chinese button....................... 121
Double knife lanyard knot 124
    Tool lanyard 126
Turk's head (4-lead, 3-bight)... 127
    Turk's head (4/3): alternate......... 129
Turk's head (3-lead, 5-bight)... 131
Solomon bar 133
Rope ladder.. 136

Glossary 138
Quick reference................................... 140
How do I?... 142
Index... 143
Acknowledgments............................... 144

INTRODUCTION

People have been making cordage from animal skin and intestine, fibers, and plant material since the beginning of recorded history. Early uses included making shelters, weaving, fishing, and tethering animals. The methods shown, in most cases, are but one way of tying the knots; with practice you may develop other methods, or learn new ones from fellow enthusiasts. Where practical, the tying processes in this book progress from left to right, and turns and rotations are clockwise, or away from you.

HOW TO USE THIS BOOK

Divided into sections by knot type, this book is a collection of practical knots. Some you might simply want to tie for decoration. Similar knots —in a progression from simple to more complex—are presented together. To help determine which type of knot will best suit the task, each knot includes an explanation about what it can be used for, and how difficult untying might be.

Icons
Icons included with each knot indicate suggested use. Some knots have broad applications; others are quite specialized.

 General   Fishing

 Camping   Sailing

 Climbing   Scouting

Star rating
Numbers indicate level of difficulty or complexity of the knot shown.

Easy   Intermediate   Advanced

Directional arrows
Arrows placed on the step-by-step photographs show the path of cord movement. They are included to reinforce the text.

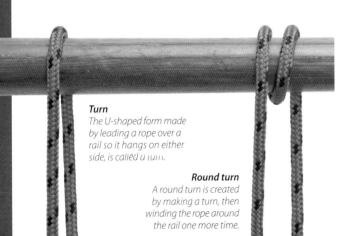

Turn
The U-shaped form made by leading a rope over a rail so it hangs on either side, is called a turn.

Round turn
A round turn is created by making a turn, then winding the rope around the rail one more time.

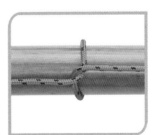

Half hitch
A half hitch is formed when rope is passed around a rail, then either under, or both under and over, itself.

Two half hitches
Two half hitches that are connected and placed directly beside each other make a clove hitch (p. 72).

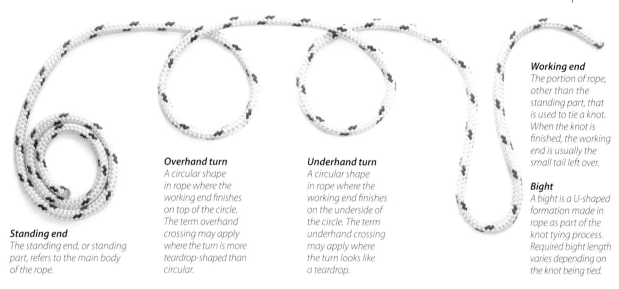

Working end
The portion of rope, other than the standing part, that is used to tie a knot. When the knot is finished, the working end is usually the small tail left over.

Bight
A bight is a U-shaped formation made in rope as part of the knot tying process. Required bight length varies depending on the knot being tied.

Standing end
The standing end, or standing part, refers to the main body of the rope.

Overhand turn
A circular shape in rope where the working end finishes on top of the circle. The term overhand crossing may apply where the turn is more teardrop-shaped than circular.

Underhand turn
A circular shape in rope where the working end finishes on the underside of the circle. The term underhand crossing may apply where the turn looks like a teardrop.

ROPE BASICS

Laid rope is the name given to cordage where the strands—usually three—wind in either a right-handed or left-handed direction. Most braided cordage contains an inner core and an outer layer. The outer component is usually composed of 16 or more woven elements, and the core, the strongest part, is made up of about eight loosely plaited strands.

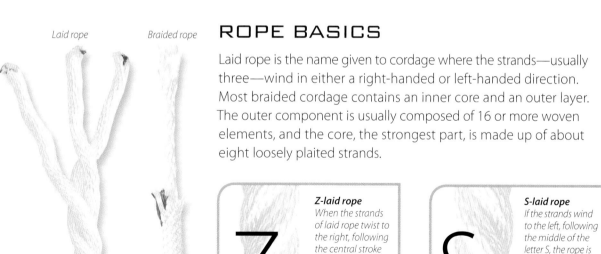

Laid rope

Braided rope

Z-laid rope
When the strands of laid rope twist to the right, following the central stroke of the letter Z, the rope is said to be Z-laid. This is the most common form of laid rope.

S-laid rope
If the strands wind to the left, following the middle of the letter S, the rope is said to be S-laid. This type of rope is less common and is usually reserved for special purposes.

TYPES OF CORDAGE

Rope has undergone major changes since the days of natural fibers. Cotton, flax, jute, sisal, coir, hemp, and manila have given way to synthetics that are strong and resistant to rot and shrinkage. Today, polyester is the most common of the plaited and braided ropes. It is often combined with other fibers to produce ropes of extremely high strength and low stretch. Other synthetic materials include polypropylene and polyethylene, which are most frequently used in the manufacture of laid rope.

Rope care

- Keep rope clean: wash to remove salt and any abrasive matter.
- Avoid abrasion: don't lead rope through sand, or over rock, unprotected corners, and edges.
- Synthetic ropes deteriorate with ultraviolet exposure: store out of direct sunlight.
- Natural fiber ropes can rot: do not store in wet or damp conditions.
- Whip, tie, or heat-seal rope ends to prevent fraying.

	Strength	Stretch	UV Resistance	Float	Handling/Tying
Coir	Poor–low	Considerable	Good	Yes / no	Good
Hemp	Low	Considerable	Good	No	Good
Sisal	Low	Considerable	Good	No	Medium–good
Manila	Low	Moderate	Very good	No	Difficult
Nylon	High	Considerable	Low	No	Good
Polyester laid	Medium–high	Moderate	Very good	No	Good
Polyester braid	High	Low–moderate	Very good	No	Very good
Polypropylene multifilament	Medium	Moderate	Poor	Yes	Very good
Polypropylene shattered film	Medium	Moderate	Good	Yes	Difficult–good
Polyethylene (Silver rope)	Medium	Moderate	Good	Yes	Medium–good
Dyneema®, Spectra® exotics	Very high	Almost nil	Good–low	No	Specialist use

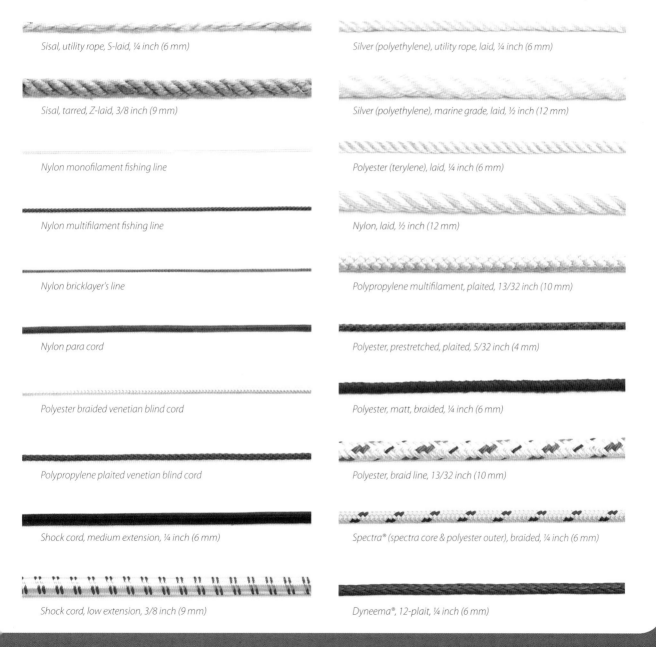

Sisal, utility rope, S-laid, ¼ inch (6 mm)

Silver (polyethylene), utility rope, laid, ¼ inch (6 mm)

Sisal, tarred, Z-laid, 3/8 inch (9 mm)

Silver (polyethylene), marine grade, laid, ½ inch (12 mm)

Nylon monofilament fishing line

Polyester (terylene), laid, ¼ inch (6 mm)

Nylon multifilament fishing line

Nylon, laid, ½ inch (12 mm)

Nylon bricklayer's line

Polypropylene multifilament, plaited, 13/32 inch (10 mm)

Nylon para cord

Polyester, prestretched, plaited, 5/32 inch (4 mm)

Polyester braided venetian blind cord

Polyester, matt, braided, ¼ inch (6 mm)

Polypropylene plaited venetian blind cord

Polyester, braid line, 13/32 inch (10 mm)

Shock cord, medium extension, ¼ inch (6 mm)

Spectra® (spectra core & polyester outer), braided, ¼ inch (6 mm)

Shock cord, low extension, 3/8 inch (9 mm)

Dyneema®, 12-plait, ¼ inch (6 mm)

TOOLS

The most obvious tool for a person handling rope is a sharp knife. However, a knife is sometimes regarded as something to be used only in an emergency—a good quality side cutter is a more useful tool, as it should sever the rope or strand in one go. For very thick rope, there may be no substitute for a sharp knife, and exotic fiber ropes require a special knife (with a partly serrated blade), available from marine stores. Other useful tools include: a hollow or Swedish fid; a wooden fid; a marlinspike; a small engineer's, shoemaker's, or cabinetmaker's hammer; an awl or spike; waxed polyester whipping twine; electrician's PVC stretchy tape; and a cigarette lighter or a hot knife for sealing.

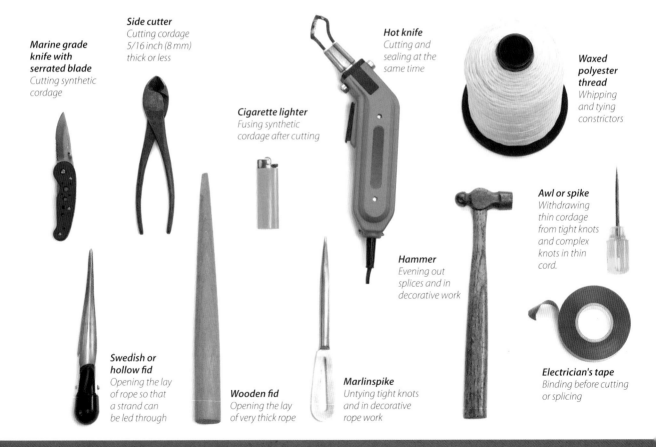

Marine grade knife with serrated blade
Cutting synthetic cordage

Side cutter
Cutting cordage 5/16 inch (8 mm) thick or less

Cigarette lighter
Fusing synthetic cordage after cutting

Hot knife
Cutting and sealing at the same time

Waxed polyester thread
Whipping and tying constrictors

Awl or spike
Withdrawing thin cordage from tight knots and complex knots in thin cord.

Hammer
Evening out splices and in decorative work

Swedish or hollow fid
Opening the lay of rope so that a strand can be led through

Wooden fid
Opening the lay of very thick rope

Marlinspike
Untying tight knots and in decorative rope work

Electrician's tape
Binding before cutting or splicing

CUTTING & SEALING

Before cutting rope with anything other than a hot knife, use knots or tape to stop the lay or braid from fraying. Tie a knot either side of where it is to be cut.

If using a knife, check that it is sharp. Alternatively, tape either side of the cut for thick rope, or tape once and cut through the center of the tape.

1 Tie a tight constrictor knot (pp. 28–9) on either side of where the rope is to be cut.

1 Make about three tight windings with electrician's tape at the site of the cut. For thick cordage, tape on either side of the cut.

1 Hold the rope above the cigarette lighter flame, not in it. Cautiously dab the end with moistened fingers or a wet sponge to tidy the edges.

2 Cut with a side cutter, or place the rope on a piece of wood and cut it with a very sharp knife.

2 Use a side cutter, or place the rope on wood and cut with a sharp knife. Press hard and cut through the center of the tape.

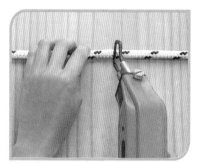

2 Alternatively, if you have access to a hot knife, cut the rope against a piece of wood. Cut thick rope in four- or five-second time segments.

WHIPPING

Whipping is the traditional method used to finish the end of a piece of rope, or its individual strands, so that it doesn't unlay, or come apart. Also, some knots can loosen when the load is removed or the rope is shaken. If the working end is whipped to the standing part, this will prevent the knot from coming undone. For whippings in the end of rope, it is usually best to begin near the end and work in the direction of the standing part. The recommended length for whipping is around one-and-a-half times the diameter of the rope, but this may be varied according to use or aesthetics.

COMMON WHIPPING

This is the quickest and most secure whipping. Both ends of the twine are tucked securely beneath the windings. It needs two lengths of twine: one about 3 feet (1 m) long for the whipping, and a shorter one, middled to form a bight, for the pull-through.

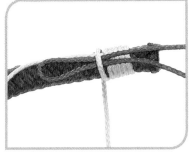

2 Wind about half way. Install the pull-through so that additional bindings will cover all but the end of the bight.

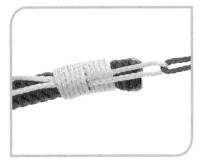

4 Maintain tension on the twine, and tug on the pull-through to draw the whipping under the bindings.

1 Make a turn around the end of the rope with the twine, and tightly bind along the rope and over the tail.

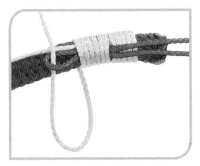

3 Continue binding tightly. When finished, pass the working end through the bight.

5 Trim the ends about 1/8 inch (3 mm) from the binding and fuse close to the binding with a cigarette lighter.

FRENCH WHIPPING

French whipping is a succession of tight half hitches. It produces an attractive spiral pattern. In thin cord, it can be used to cover a handle to improve its grip.

WEST COUNTRY WHIPPING

West country whipping secures each turn as you go. Should the whipping chafe at one point, it is less likely that the whole lot will come undone.

1 Tie an overhand knot (p. 17) around the rope with twine, so that the working end is proceeding in the direction that you are about to bind.

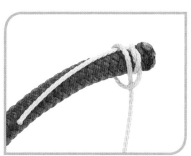

2 Tie a half hitch (p. 6) to bind the tail to the rope. Push the hitch tightly against the overhand knot. Continue tying half hitches. The tail can be trimmed after five half hitches.

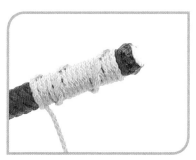

3 Make the last two half hitches with an extra tuck each, as in the multiple overhand knot (p. 17). Trim 1/8 inch (3 mm) from the binding and fuse with a cigarette lighter.

1 Start with 3 feet (1 m) of twine. At its center, tie an overhand knot (p. 17) around the rope. Tie all following overhand knots in the same way as the first—either left over, or right over.

2 Turn the rope over and tie an overhand knot on the opposite side to the first. Continue alternating so that the knots progress along each side of the rope without overlapping.

3 Finish each side with an extra turn around itself, as in the multiple overhand knot (p. 17). Trim the ends 1/8 inch (3 mm) from the knot and fuse with a cigarette lighter.

COILING ROPE

The easiest way to store or carry a length of rope is to coil it. However, simply gathering overhand turns can put a twist in the rope: a clockwise twist if you are right handed, a counterclockwise twist if left. The methods demonstrated here gather the coils with the right hand and collect them in the left.

1 Depending on the thickness and length of the rope, form a suitably sized overhand turn. Ensure that the short end hangs below the bottom of the turn so that it won't slip inside and tangle.

2 Pick up the hanging part with the thumb and index finger. As you raise it, turn the hanging part toward you with a clockwise turn of the wrist. Place this underhand turn next to the previous one in the left hand.

3 Make alternate overhand and underhand turns. If the rope is twisted and it is not convenient to shake it out, gather an over- or underhand turn or two out of order to accommodate the twist temporarily.

WRAPPED COIL

This coiling technique is particularly suitable for long-term storage or transport. It takes longer to tie than other methods but there is little chance of other ropes or coils tangling with it.

1 Tie a reef knot (p. 22–3) at the top, with each working end twice the length of the coil's circumference.

2 Wind the right working end over and around—and the left, under and around—to the bottom of the coil.

3 Where the working ends meet, tie another reef knot, so that the two knots are at opposite sides of the coil.

BUNDLED COIL

This is a quick method that can be easily undone, to secure a coil that can be tossed into a trailer, stored in a locker, or hung by the tail. It can also be used for stowing a jib sheet or other sailing rope, and for securing the unused portion of a rope when either the tail or the standing part is fixed.

1 Leave a working tail up to one-and-a-half times the circumference of the coil. Elongate the coil and at about one-third down from the top, wind the tail around the coil moving upward and over itself.

2 Make about four neat windings that do not overlap. Form a bight in the tail, pull it through the coil, and slip it over and around the top of the coil. Pull on the tail.

3 The coil can be hung on a peg, or tied by the tail to a rail using a clove hitch (p. 72) or a slipped overhand knot (p. 18). To undo the coil, slide the bight back over the top and through the coil.

DOUBLE SLIP COIL

The double slip method allows for very quick access to the coil. It works in a similar manner to the highwayman's hitch (pp. 80–1). If the coil does not need to be hung, or is to be placed over a peg, simply pull the slip overhand knot tight at the end of Step 2, and do not continue with Step 3.

1 Leaving a tail about one-and-a-half times the circumference of the coil, form a bight with its center about two hand spans from the top of the coil.

2 Pass the bight over and around the coil and tie a slipped overhand knot (p. 18). Hold both the coil and the overhand knot together in one hand.

3 Form a new bight in the tail, lead it into the coil, up, over, and to the right of the first bight, then under itself. Tighten. Hang the coil by the first bight. To release, unhang and pull on the tail.

STOPPERS

Stopper knots of the simple kind shown here are tied to prevent rope, line, or string slipping through a hole or other narrow opening. They also stop cord ends fraying. The overhand knot is the simplest, and is the starting point for many other knots. Try a multiple overhand knot when a bulkier stopper is required. The figure-of-eight knot, the easiest of the three to untie, is often used when sailing.

OVERHAND KNOT

- MULTIPLE OVERHAND
- SLIPPED OVERHAND

The simplest knot that can be tied, the overhand knot is the starting point for many other knots. On its own, the overhand knot works as a stopper, but when pulled tight, may be difficult to untie. The multiple overhand knot is more easily loosened. The slipped overhand knot can be released quickly, but be careful how you use it, as it may shake loose.

Pass the working end over and through the center of the turn, from back to front. Pull on both ends to tighten the knot.

With the standing part of the rope in the left hand and the working end in the right, make an overhand turn.

MULTIPLE OVERHAND

Feed the working end around the turn several times.

Begin as for Step 1 of the overhand knot, but before tightening, feed the working end around the turn another one, two, or three times.

If you need to untie a multiple overhand knot, try flexing it to loosen it.

The more times you take the working end around the turn, the more you will have to manipulate the knot when tightening to make it even and tidy.

Wind the bight, but not the end itself, over and through the center of the turn.

SLIPPED OVERHAND

Make an overhand turn as in Step 1 of the overhand knot (p. 17), but with sufficient length in your right hand to make a generous bight.

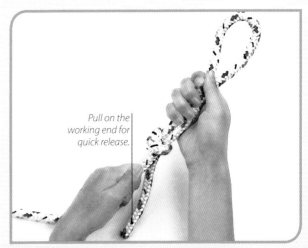

Pull on the working end for quick release.

Tighten by pulling on both the standing part and the bight. To undo, pull on the working end and the knot will slip apart easily.

FIGURE-OF-EIGHT KNOT

Deriving its name from the shape of the numeral 8, the figure-of-eight knot is almost as simple to tie as the overhand knot (p. 17). It can be tied quickly at the end of a rope. When pulled tight and put under strain, the figure-of-eight knot is much easier to untie than the overhand knot. For any application using pulleys or block and tackle, it is the best knot for preventing rope from running out through a block.

With the standing part in the left hand and the working end in the right, make an overhand turn. Tuck the working end behind the standing part and bring it forward.

Follow the shape of the numeral 8 and lead the working end through the overhand turn.

Direct the working end through the turn, from front to back, and pull on both ends. If it has been pulled very tight and is difficult to untie, bend the knot slightly to loosen.

BINDINGS

Binding knots are tied in a single piece of cordage around bundles of objects, such as coiled rope strands and bag necks, to hold them together or seal the opening. Bindings and lashings perform similar tasks, but bindings are temporary, can be used on pliable materials, and have just one or two confining turns rather than multiple windings. Bindings should not be used as bends to join two lengths of cordage, nor as hitches to attach load-bearing rope to an object.

SURGEON'S KNOT: BINDING

As the name suggests, this knot gained its name on the operating table. It is simple to tie and works particularly well in suture material and thin twine. The first half of the knot is capable of keeping tension on the object until the second half is secured. This binding version of a surgeon's knot is a variation on the surgeon's knot bend (p. 58) and has one extra winding in the second stage. When tied using fine line, it will be difficult to untie and may need to be cut.

2 What began as your left working end is now your right. Wind the new right working end over and around the left, and continue to make a second winding.

1 Pass the cord around the item or bundle and wind the left end over and around the right end—as for the first half of a reef knot (pp. 22–3)—twice, then tighten.

In some applications, a third winding is added to each half of the knot.

3 Tighten so that the two halves of the knot lie evenly side by side. Fine or slippery cord may slip slightly until the second stage of the knot is firmed.

BINDINGS

REEF KNOT
• GRANNY KNOT

The reef knot is easy to tie and untie, and is a very useful knot for tying bundles and securing parcels. The name probably comes from its use in reducing sail in bad weather—"reefing down"—by tying reef points around the excess sail. It must be tightened against a surface for stability. The granny knot is usually a reef knot gone wrong, and shown only so that you will recognize it. It is not reliable and when it does work, it is hard to untie. Of the two knots, the reef knot is far superior.

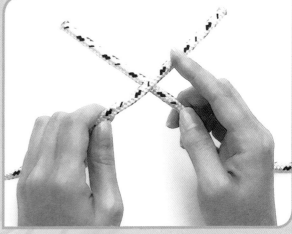

1 With an end of rope in each hand, lay the left working end over the right.

2 Wind the left end around the right end and bring it back to the front. What were once the left and right ends of rope are now reversed.

*Left over right,
then right over left*

3 Do the same as for Step 2, except wind the new right working end over the left. The rule is to wind the left end in the first half of the knot, and the right in the second.

GRANNY KNOT

5 For the granny knot, proceed as for the reef knot to the end of Step 2. Then instead of Step 3, wind the left over the right again.

4 Draw both sides of the rope tight to complete the knot.

6 Pull very tight. When the surface of the rope is slippery or smooth, the granny knot has a tendency to slip, especially when not pulled taut against a flat surface.

BINDINGS

POLE LASHING

Pole lashing, also known as the scaffold hitch and Oklahoma hitch, will bind long thin objects of assorted sizes and profiles. When used as quick lashing, the ends pulling through their respective bights work as a tackle, helping to draw the bundle up tightly before it is secured with a binding knot, such as a reef knot (pp. 22–3). If the shape of the bundle changes during tightening, the hitch can be adjusted. A pair of pole lashings can hold glued items firmly until dry. As a plank sling, it makes a quick and simple temporary shelf for the garage.

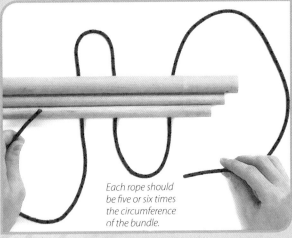

Each rope should be five or six times the circumference of the bundle.

1 To bind a bundle, you will need two lengths of rope—one for a pole lashing at each end. Arrange the rope on the ground in a Z pattern, and lay one end of the bundle on top.

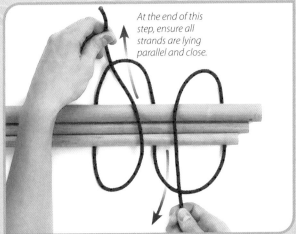

At the end of this step, ensure all strands are lying parallel and close.

2 There is now a bight on either side of the bundle. Pass each end of rope across the top of the bundle and through the opposite bight. Pull on the ends to tighten.

Reef knot reminder: left over right, then right over left.

3 Secure the lashing with a binding knot, such as the reef knot (pp. 22–3). With the lashing pulled tight, lead the left working end over the right.

PLANK SLING

Position bights opposite each other on the plank edges.

5 When suspending a plank, arrange the bights at the edges of the plank, with all parts of the rope lying flat on the plank. A bowline (pp. 36–7) can be tied to join both ends.

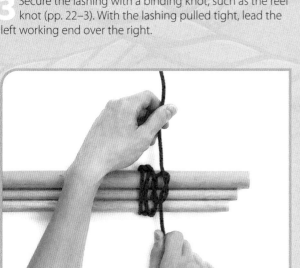

4 Take the right working end over the left and pull tight. Repeat Steps 1–4 at the other end of the bundle. A bundle may splay apart unless secured in two places.

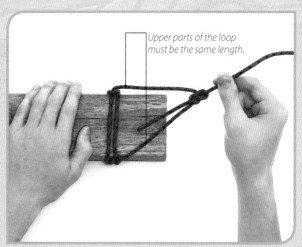

Upper parts of the loop must be the same length.

6 Make sure that the two upper parts of the loop are the same length, so that the bowline is centered and the plank will sit level when suspended.

BAG KNOT
• SLIPPED BAG KNOT

Well suited to securing the neck of a cloth bag, the bag knot is similar to the constrictor knot (pp. 28–9), so study both carefully—it is easy to confuse the two. A bag knot is held secure by the friction between the rope and the bag itself, therefore it may not work well using slippery rope. For small bags and fine cord, use a slipped bag knot to save time untying a tiny, tight knot or to prevent the bag from being nicked by a tool used to pick the knot apart.

1 Make a turn over the gathered neck of the sack, placing the working end to the right of the standing part.

2 Bring the working end to the top left, crossing it over the standing part.

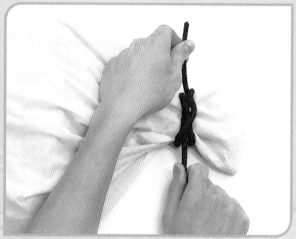

4 Lay the working end diagonally right across the knot and tuck it under the first turn made around the sack, feeding it from right to left. Pull tight.

3 Feed the working end around the back of the sack and place it to the left of the standing part.

SLIPPED BAG KNOT

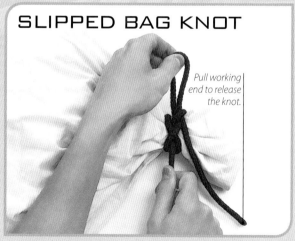

Pull working end to release the knot.

5 For a slipped version of the knot, make a bight in the working end before tucking it under the turn in Step 4. Pull tight. To release, simply pull on the working end.

BINDINGS

CONSTRICTOR KNOT

• SLIPPED CONSTRICTOR KNOT

This is a useful knot for tying a bundle. It is similar to the bag knot (pp. 26–7), but relies on the friction between the parts of the rope itself, rather than between the rope and the surface. The constrictor can often be used instead of a clove hitch (p. 72): the constrictor is more secure but can be more difficult to untie. When tied in a colored thread, it can mark a particular point in a complicated knot.

1 Working from left to right, wind the working end over and around the bundle, forming a turn.

2 Cross the working end diagonally left over the standing part, and wind it around the bundle again.

To sever a constrictor knot, cut through this top turn with a knife. The lower turns protect the bundle from being nicked.

Ease the two halves of the knot together and pull tightly on both ends.

4 Take the working end over the top of the first turn that was formed and pass it underneath. The working end should now be in the center, between the two turns.

3 Proceeding from left to right, take the working end under the diagonal crossing. You have now formed a loose clove hitch.

SLIPPED CONSTRICTOR KNOT

Tug on the working end to quickly release the knot.

5 For the slipped version, begin with Steps 1–3 of the constrictor knot. Make a bight in the working end and complete Step 4 using this bight.

BINDINGS

BOTTLE SLING

The bottle sling, also called the jug sling, is a little more involved than some other binding knots. The knot provides a carry handle for a bottle, or any item, with a flange or shoulder large enough to prevent the knot from slipping off. The bottle sling provides an artistic way to display decorative bottles and lipped vases, and allows drinks to be hung over the side of a boat to cool in the water. The knot should be laid out spaciously on a surface, as the procedure is as much visual as it is mechanical. This example requires about 5 feet (1.5 m) of cord.

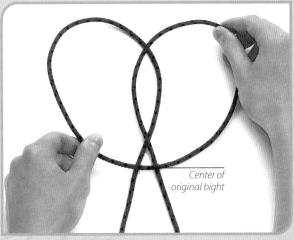

Center of original bight

2 Partially overlap the right ear over the left, so that the center of the original bight remains below the lower intersection of the ears.

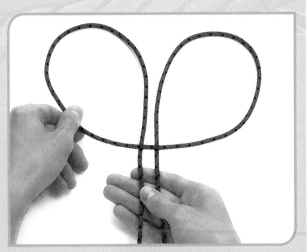

1 Middle the cord and place the resulting bight flat on the table. Draw the bight down over the standing parts to make two evenly sized "ears."

Keep the knot flat on the table.

3 Holding the pattern in place on the table with one hand, draw the center of the original bight under the knot at the point of the lower intersection of the ears.

Draw the original bight up through the overlap of the ears.

4 Now bring the center of the original bight up through the space formed by the overlapping ears, to make a new bight at the top.

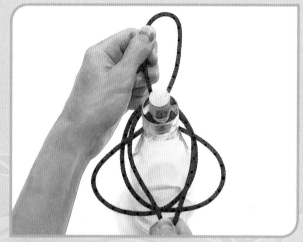

6 Lift the knot carefully and place the hole over the neck of the bottle. Tighten by pulling on the upper bight and evenly on the pair of ends.

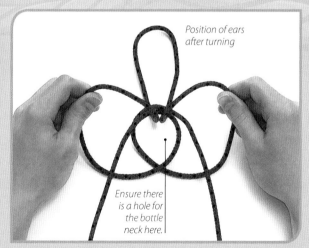

Position of ears after turning

Ensure there is a hole for the bottle neck here.

5 Using both hands, turn the ears and center part over simultaneously, with the top moving away from you. The top of the ears now finish at the bottom of the pattern.

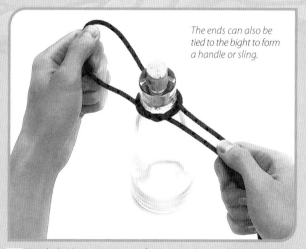

The ends can also be tied to the bight to form a handle or sling.

7 Work the knot to a snug fit around the neck of the bottle. The ends can be tied together to make a second handle, using a fisherman's knot (p. 56) or figure-of-eight bend (p. 55).

BINDINGS

TRANSOM KNOT

The transom knot is used to tie two poles together at right angles. It is similar to the constrictor knot (pp. 28–9). While not as strong or rigid as the square lashing (pp. 93–4) or diagonal lashing (pp. 95–6), it is quicker to tie and easier to remove. This makes it particularly suitable for light jobs with many knots to be tied. The knot can be reinforced with a second transom knot tied at 90 degrees to the first. Using less cord than a lashing, the transom knot is good for small, fiddly tasks. A drop of glue applied where the cord crosses will make the knot more secure.

2 Firm the knot slightly. It should resemble two half hitches. Lead the working end over and under the right-hand portion of the first diagonal.

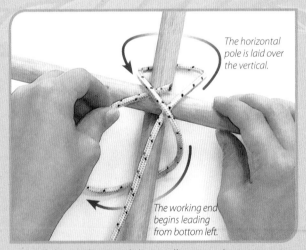

The horizontal pole is laid over the vertical.

The working end begins leading from bottom left.

1 Lead the working end diagonally across the intersection, left behind the vertical pole, diagonally across again, left behind the vertical pole, and under the last diagonal crossing.

To double the strength, tie a second transom knot behind the first.

3 Pull the standing and working ends in opposite directions. If required, turn the structure over, rotate it 90 degrees, and with another piece of cord, tie the knot again.

LOOPS

Loop knots are closed bights tied either in the bight, which requires no access to the ends, or at the end of a rope. Single, double, or multiple loops can be formed. Fixed loops do not change size. Running loops are tied, then pulled tight around an object. When rope must be reused, select a knot that is easily untied. Some that are hard to untie after loading particularly suit disposable fine line and shock cord. Having an independent structure, fixed loops can be used for handholds, footholds, and reusable attachment points.

Attaching an item to a rope; making a fixed loop; suspending an object from two points

LOOPS

FIGURE-OF-EIGHT LOOP

This is a fixed single loop tied in the same way as the figure-of-eight knot (p. 19) but with a bight formed in the working end. It can also be tied along the length of rope—called a figure-of-eight on the bight—and can take a load on one end, both ends in parallel, or both ends pulling in different directions. Items to be attached to the loop can be threaded into the bight before tying, or cow hitched to the loop after tying.

Continue the figure-of-eight pattern and pass the loop, or the item that was threaded into it earlier, through the turn, from front to back.

Form a bight and make an overhand crossing. The bight will become the loop. Lead the loop around behind the standing part and the working end.

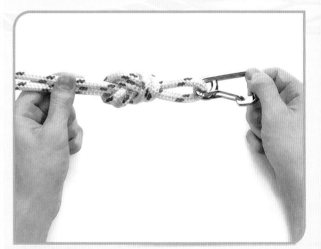

Pull the loop tight. A load may be applied to both ends or to the long standing part only. The loop is very secure but can be harder to untie than the figure-of-eight knot.

SURGEON'S LOOP

The surgeon's loop is a fixed loop that holds well in thin, smooth cord, fishing line, and shock cord. It is, in fact, a triple overhand knot tied with a bight. Single and double overhand versions are tied in exactly the same way but might not be as secure. It is a difficult knot to untie once loaded, so is best used for permanent loops or where the line will be cut once the loop is no longer needed. Wetting fine line will make it easier to work the knot tight.

Make a second and a third winding.

Wind the bight through the turn twice more to tie a triple overhand knot. For shock cord, the two extra windings should suffice. Three is best for fishing line.

Form a bight and make a loose overhand knot.

Begin with a bight twice the length of the loop that you wish to make. Form an overhand turn in the bight and tie an overhand knot (p. 17).

Work spiral section tight and even.

Hold the bight in one hand and the standing parts in the other: pull to firm the knot. It is important to the integrity of the knot to achieve an even, spiral appearance.

BOWLINE
- DOUBLE BOWLINE
- WATER BOWLINE
- BOWLINE: ALTERNATE

The bowline, a fixed loop, is a practical knot that is especially useful on a boat or dockside. The double bowline is used for very slippery rope, and the water bowline in cordage that may tend to jam when wet. Two ropes of different type and diameter may be joined by tying a bowline in each with the loops interlocked.

Begin with a working part twice the length of the circumference of the loop you wish to make.

Make a small overhand turn and lead the working end through it from underneath. The size of the finished loop depends on how much of the working end is pulled through.

Make sure the working end is led correctly through the turn.

Having decided on the size of the loop, pass the working end behind the standing part, up and to the front, then lead it back through the turn, parallel with itself.

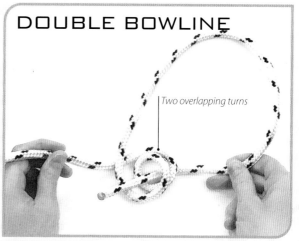

DOUBLE BOWLINE

Two overlapping turns

For a double bowline, make two overlapping overhand turns instead of the single turn in Step 1, and pass the working end up and through both turns.

Grasp the working end and its parallel part in one hand, the standing part in the other, and pull. If the knot falls apart, the working end was led incorrectly in Step 1.

Continue the working end behind the standing part as in Step 2, then back and parallel with itself through both turns.

LOOPS

Tighten as in Step 3, and take the slack out of the knot. If the loop is now too large, ease it out on the parallel part and remove the slack by pulling on the working end.

Continue leading the working end behind the standing part, up and to the front, then back through each turn, following the same pattern as in Step 2.

WATER BOWLINE

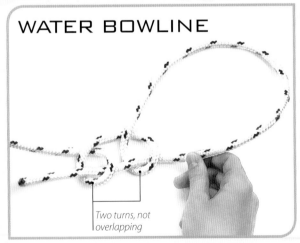

Two turns, not overlapping

For a water bowline, begin with Step 1, but make two distinct overhand turns and do not overlap them. Lead the working end up through each turn separately.

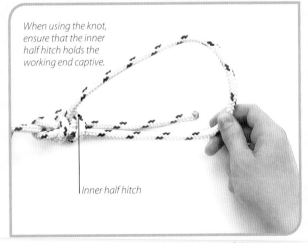

When using the knot, ensure that the inner half hitch holds the working end captive.

Inner half hitch

Tighten as in Step 3. Feed the slack out of the inner half hitch and transfer it to the loop. The loop can be adjusted if necessary as in Step 6.

L
O
O
P
S

BOWLINE: ALTERNATE

Use this method to tie a bowline directly around an object.

Tie an overhand knot, making sure the working end passes over the standing part and then under it. The working end must be long enough to allow a firm handhold.

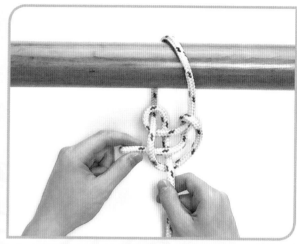

Take the working end behind the standing part from left to right, through the loop from front to back, then back over the standing part and under itself.

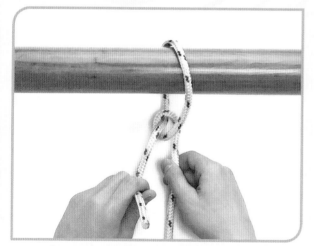

Capsize the overhand knot by pulling the working end downward until it is straight. The standing part forms a turn around it, as in Step 2.

Pull the working end upward and away so that it slides under the bottom of the turn and pops inside it. Pull it around the back and to the right to sit inside the loop.

L O O P S

BOWLINE ON THE BIGHT

This is a fixed double loop tied either in the bight or with a bight formed at the end of the rope. The parallel loops can function as two single loops or one thicker, stronger loop, and the load can be applied to one or both standing parts. Bar and brewery workers once used this bowline for hoisting and lowering barrels off trucks and into cellars. Like the Spanish bowline (pp. 50–1), it can be utilized to lift irregularly shaped objects.

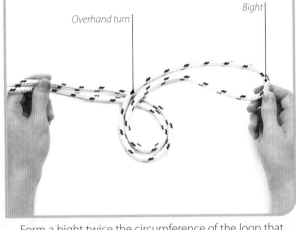

Overhand turn   *Bight*

Form a bight twice the circumference of the loop that you wish to create. The bight itself is the working end. Make a small overhand turn.

Make sure the working end is led correctly through the turn.

Lead the bight through the turn, from back to front. The portion that is not drawn through the turn will become the loop.

Bight will move this way in Step 4.

As with the bowline (pp. 36–7), take the end of the bight up and around behind the standing part.

Pull on the standing parts and the lower, or bight, side of the loop to tighten. You may have to feed some of the bight excess into the loop itself.

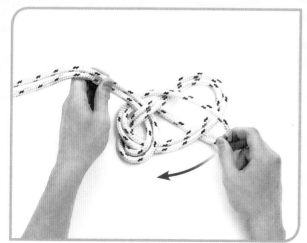

Open out the bight and slip it over and around the whole knot, so that it holds the two standing ends captive.

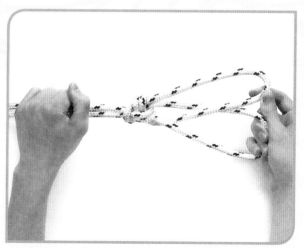

The two loops can be used separately or as one. If the knot is loosened and adjusted, one loop can be made proportionally larger or smaller than the other.

Attaching a swivel to fishing line; tethering a dinghy; making a loop in shock cord

ANGLER'S LOOP

The angler's loop is a fixed single loop normally tied in an end. It makes a secure, permanent loop that holds well under load in fishing line and shock cord. It is important, however, to pull the knot up tight before use. In thin cord, fishing line, or shock cord, the angler's loop is difficult or impossible to untie and is best used where line can be cut once the loop is no longer needed. A clip, snap hook, or other item can be threaded into the bight at Step 1, or cow hitched to the loop later.

Direction of rotation in Step 2

Begin with a working part twice the length of the loop you wish to make. Make an underhand turn and then form a bight in the working end.

Rotate the bight right to left, then lead it through the turn from front to back. The bight, which is now the slipped portion, will become the loop.

LOOPS

Overhand knot

If the working end is excessively long, pull the extra cord into the loop. Work it out through the overhand knot and into the standing end.

Slide the working end under both strands of the loop, from right to left.

Thumb inserted to show channel the working end passes through in Step 5.

Lead the working end around behind the standing part, adjacent to the lower portion of the overhand knot.

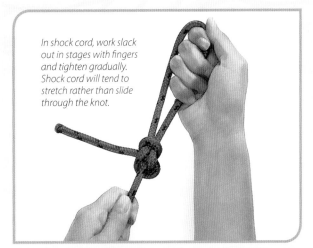

In shock cord, work slack out in stages with fingers and tighten gradually. Shock cord will tend to stretch rather than slide through the knot.

Tighten the knot by pulling on the loop, the standing part, and the working end. Pull hard on the loop and standing part to complete, particularly in shock cord, which stretches.

LOOPS

ALPINE BUTTERFLY KNOT

The alpine butterfly knot, or loop, also known as the lineman's loop, is an easily untied fixed single loop. It suits fishing line, cord, and thin rope, but is awkward to tie in thick rope. It can be loaded on either end or on the loop, so in a hoisting line, it provides both a load attachment loop and a ground control line. The knot can extend a damaged rope's life when tied with the weakened section in an unloaded loop.

Lay the left standing part diagonally over the turn.

Winding away from you, left to right, make a round turn and one extra turn around the left hand. Place the left standing part over the first turn and secure it with the thumb.

Extend this turn to create a long bight.

Pick up the bottom of the left round turn and, allowing the left standing part to run around the hand, extend a bight to at least triple the size of the turn.

Secure the two standing parts together with the left thumb, grasp the loop with the right hand, and pull to tighten.

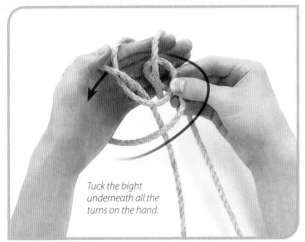

Tuck the bight underneath all the turns on the hand.

Lead the newly extended bight to the right and tuck it, right to left, under all the turns that are wound around the hand to form a loop.

Work the knot into a tidy shape at the base of the loop.

The two standing parts can now be spread to restore the function of a continuous rope. You may need to work the outer turns of the knot inward and pull on the loop to tidy it.

LOOPS

BLOOD LOOP DROPPER KNOT

The blood loop dropper knot is a fixed loop that holds well in slippery materials, such as shock cord and fishing line. Its tight wrapping turns identify it as a member of the blood knot family, which includes the blood knot (p. 57). The loop is perfect for attaching droppers—separate lines with a hook or sinker, which give the knot its name—to a single line. Wetting fine line will make it easier to tighten the knot. When making a series of dropper loops, tie the loop furthest from the working end first.

Form an overhand turn at the required place along a line; secure it with your thumb and index finger. The size of the turn depends on the number of windings you make in Step 2.

Tie a multiple overhand knot with four, six, or eight windings. The thinner and more slippery the line, the greater the number required to make the knot secure.

Note that in doing this, half a turn is lost from the left part of the windings and another is added to the right.

Pick up the bottom center point of the original turn and lead it up through the hole to form a loop. Check that the hole is actually at the center of the windings.

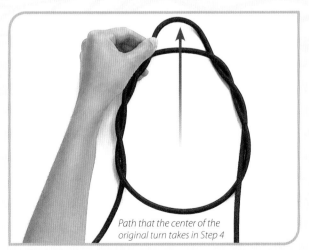

Path that the center of the original turn takes in Step 4

Find the center point of the windings and draw it slightly away from the turn to make a hole. Keep the hole open.

Secure the loop by pulling three ways: on the loop and the two portions of line. If necessary, slide the windings neatly up to the loop.

LOOPS

ARBOR KNOT

This knot makes a running loop that can be put around a post, spar, or drum, and tightened by pulling on the standing part. It is one of several arbor knots that can be used to attach fishing line to a reel, or arbor. This particular running loop can be collapsed without having to be untied: once the item in the loop is removed, simply pull on the standing part and the loop slips back through the knot, which collapses. Never use a running loop in any situation where it could get caught around a person's fingers or limbs.

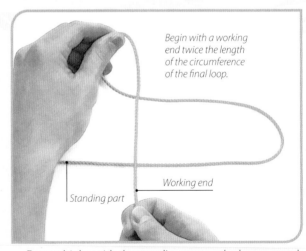

Begin with a working end twice the length of the circumference of the final loop.

Working end

Standing part

Form a bight, with the standing part as the lower strand and the working end above it. Make an overhand turn in the working end and lead it down over the standing part.

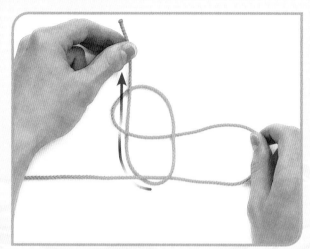

Tuck the working end under the standing part, lead it upward under the lower part of the turn, and up through the center of the turn. This forms one wind.

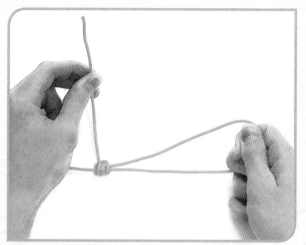

Pull on the bight and the working end to firm the windings about the standing part. Mold the turns into shape by rolling them between thumb and index finger.

Form a total of three winds, right to left.

Wind the working end around the inside of the turn and the standing part, twice more. Work from right to left, and downward at the front and upward behind.

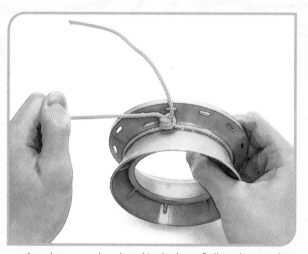

A reel can now be placed in the loop. Pull on the standing part and slide the knot hard against the reel. To remove the reel, slide the knot back along the standing part.

LOOPS

SPANISH BOWLINE

The Spanish bowline, like the bowline on the bight (pp. 40–1), is a fixed double loop tied in the bight, but with splayed loops rather than parallel ones. The size of each loop can be independently adjusted. Irregularly shaped objects can be hoisted using this knot as long as the loops are adjusted to fit snugly, so that slack isn't pulled from one loop into the other if the loops are unequally loaded. This bowline has been used in emergency rescue.

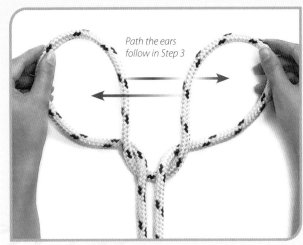

Path the ears follow in Step 3

Turn each ear over symmetrically away from you, to give the overhand intersections an extra winding.

Direction of rotation in Step 2

Form a bight in the center, or at the desired place along a length of rope, open out the bight and turn it over and away from you to create two overhand turns, or "ears."

Crossing turn

Cross the two ears, sliding the left ear under and up through the right ear. Note that a crossing turn has been formed around the two standing parts.

Keep the pattern flat on the table, and pass the fingers of each hand into their respective ears from the rear. With the left fingers, pick up the left edge of the crossing turn.

Grasp the rope here.

Continue drawing your hands apart to create a new bight in each hand. Tighten by pulling on the loops together in one hand and the standing parts in the other.

Draw it slightly into the left ear. Repeat with the right hand, picking up the right edge of the crossing turn and drawing it into the right ear.

Grasp the rope here.

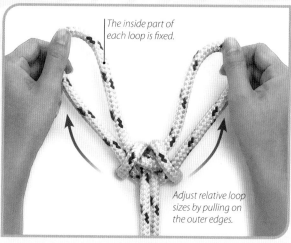

The inside part of each loop is fixed.

Adjust relative loop sizes by pulling on the outer edges.

The inside part of each loop is locked by the knot, but the outer edges can be slid to make one loop larger or smaller than the other.

LOOPS

JURY MAST KNOT

This knot allows an extra spar to be "jury rigged" as an emergency mast. The center eye sits over the end and the ropes holding the makeshift mast upright attach to the three adjustable loops. It can also be used for erecting a tent or flagpole, as long as there is a shoulder, through bolt, or other device to prevent the knot sliding down the pole. Laid flat, it is an interesting and attractive knot that can be stitched to a bag or jacket sleeve as decorative trim.

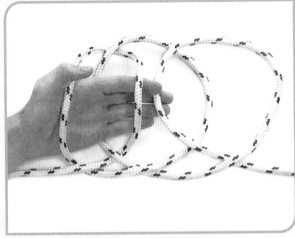

Lead the left hand into the first turn from underneath, over the left edge of the second turn, under the right edge of the first turn, and pick up the left edge of the third.

Working from left to right, make three underhand turns. The left edges of the second and third turns should overlap the right edges of the first and second turns.

With the right hand, lead over the right edge of the third turn, under the right edge of the second turn, over the left edge of the third turn, and pick up the right edge of the first.

LOOPS

Center of second turn

Draw your hands apart far enough so that two loose bights begin to form. The remainder of the knot should be circular in shape with an obvious hole in the middle.

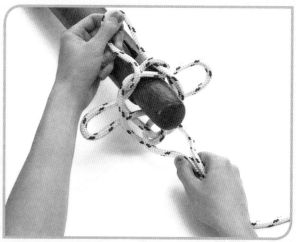

Place the knot over the end of a spar, and adjust to fit snugly. Tie both standing ends together about the spar. The three bights become attachment points for stays.

The second turn is still in the circular portion of the knot. Draw it out carefully at the top to form a third bight. Adjust the knot so that the three bights are of a similar size.

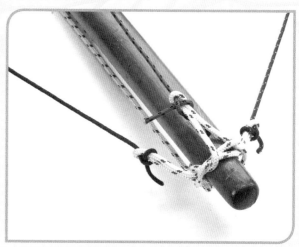

The stays—rope or wire supporting the mast—can be attached to the jury mast knot with sheet bends or double sheet bends (pp. 62–3).

BENDS

Bends join two lengths of cordage. Some bends are secure only in lines of the same size, or under constant load. Others can join lines of different sizes, or hold secure even when unloaded and shaken. A few are particularly suited to specific materials, such as shock cord. Some hitches, such as the anchor bend (pp. 76–7), are also called bends: in old sailing terminology "to bend" meant to attach a rope to an object, usually an anchor, or to join two ropes together. Such hitches should not be confused with actual bends.

FIGURE-OF-EIGHT BEND

The figure-of-eight bend is also known as a Flemish bend. It is a suitable knot for joining two lengths of cordage of the same diameter, but the bend can be rather bulky in some cordage. It is not suited to monofilament fishing line and shock cord. The tying process is simple and easy to remember, especially once you know how to tie the figure-of-eight knot, and produces a strong, reliable result.

2 Lead the second rope into the knot parallel to the first working end. Continue through the knot until the second working end emerges beside the standing part of the first.

BENDS

1 Tie a loose figure-of-eight knot (p. 19) near, but not too close to, the end of the first length of rope. Then begin doubling the knot with the second rope.

3 Make sure the knot is neat and even. Pull alternately on the standing parts and the working ends to tighten.

BENDS

FISHERMAN'S KNOT

- DOUBLE FISHERMAN'S KNOT
- BLOOD KNOT

These knots are suitable for joining two lengths of fishing line, shock cord, and thin rope of similar size and type. The fisherman's knot is also known as the angler's, English, halibut, and waterman's knot. The double fisherman's knot, which is less inclined to slip, is used by climbers, while the blood knot is mainly an angling knot.

2 Make an overhand knot with the second working end to capture the standing part of the first rope. Tie this second overhand knot in the opposite direction to the first.

1 Lead the working ends together from opposite directions and overlap them. Make an overhand knot (p.17) in one of the working ends so that the other rope is captured.

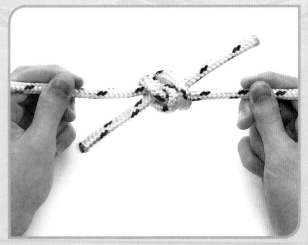

3 Pull each overhand knot tight, then draw the two together by pulling on the standing parts.

DOUBLE FISHERMAN'S KNOT

The ends should be pointing in opposite directions

4 For a more secure version of the fisherman's knot, tie a multiple overhand knot (pp. 17–18) with two windings in each working end around the other rope's standing part.

6 Repeat with the second rope around its partner, winding in the opposite direction for the same number of turns, and taking the working end back between the two ropes.

BLOOD KNOT

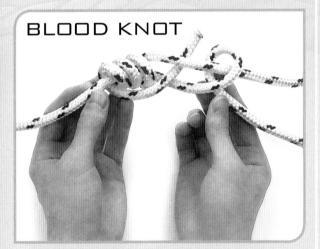

5 Begin with a slightly longer overlap than in Step 1. Wind one rope around the other four or five times. Return the working end over the windings and between the two ropes.

7 Pull on the standing parts to bring the two halves together, then firm up and neaten the knot by pulling on the working ends. Pull on the standing parts again.

BENDS

BENDS

SURGEON'S KNOT: BEND

The surgeon's knot bend, also called the ligature knot, is a variation of a reef knot (pp. 22–3). The surgeon's knot works well in sewing cotton and twine, but it should not be made with shock cord or ropes of significantly different size and texture. For greater security when using fishing line, tie the knot with three windings in Step 1 and two windings in Step 2. Although it may initially slip with fishing line, the knot becomes secure when tightened properly.

Wind this working end over and under the other one.

2 The former left working end is now at the right side of the knot. Pass this end over and under the left, winding it around just once, so it comes out the left side of the knot.

Start by winding the left working end over the right.

1 Pass the left working end over the right and wind it around as in Step 2 of a reef knot (p. 22). Continue and make a second winding in the same direction.

3 Pull tightly on both standing ends. The knot will assume a spiral appearance. The final result is a reef knot with an extra winding in the first half.

CARRICK BEND

The carrick bend can be used to join ropes of the same or slightly different sizes. Since there is not much manipulation in its tying, the knot is suited to joining large ropes. It capsizes under load but does not jam; even in large rope, a few knocks with a hammer will loosen the knot. Left flat, it can be stitched or glued onto an item as trim. Tied as for a binding knot in opposite ends of the same cord, the carrick bend forms the basis of several decorative knots, including the knife lanyard knot (pp. 118–20) and the double Chinese button (pp. 121–3).

2 Continue feeding the working end of the second rope under the upper edge of the turn, over its own standing part, then under the lower edge of the turn to exit.

Overhand crossing

1 Form an overhand crossing with one rope. Lead another rope from the opposite direction, over the turn of the first rope, under the standing part, then over the working part.

Knot capsizes when tightened.

3 Tighten the knot by alternately pulling on the working ends and the standing parts. It is normal for the knot to capsize as it is pulled tight.

BENDS

BENDS

ASHLEY'S BEND

This bend can be loaded on the working ends as well as the standing ends. It can join two lengths of rope, or, with two long working ends, provide four usable standing parts. It can therefore make a four-way tie-down with the crossing point fixed in place, so that the ropes cannot chafe or shift as they might if simply looped around each other and led away to form two right angles. The knot works well in rope, shock cord, fishing line, and twine. It holds in dissimilar materials, such as rope and shock cord, as long as they are of similar diameter.

Working end under

1 To finish the knot with four standing parts, first decide at which point along the rope you will place the knot. Take the first length of rope and form an underhand crossing.

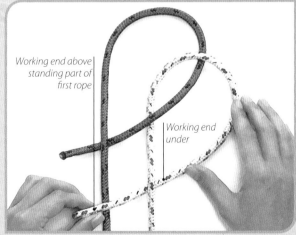

Working end above standing part of first rope

Working end under

2 Take the second rope and feed it into the loop of the crossing from underneath. Form an underhand crossing, with the working end on top of the first rope's standing part.

Ends together through center of both turns

3 Slide the two crossings closer together. Pick up both working ends in one hand and lead them down through both loops, as though completing an overhand knot.

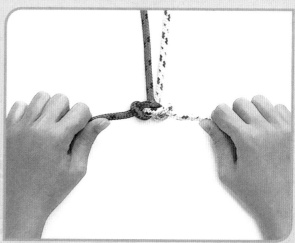

5 Pick up one standing part in each hand and pull them in opposite directions to finish tightening the knot.

4 Grasp the working ends in one hand and standing parts in the other. Pull on both pairs of ends to begin tightening the knot.

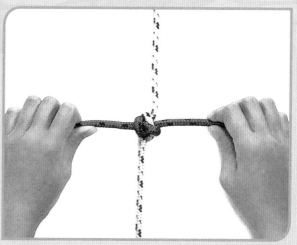

6 If four usable ends are required, the knot will need further alternate tightening to achieve uniform shape and stability. This is particularly important for shock cord.

BENDS

SHEET BEND
• DOUBLE SHEET BEND

Quick and easy to tie and untie, this is a very useful knot aboard boats, but be careful as a finger can easily be caught. Both bends can join ropes of differing sizes. The double sheet bend is less likely to shake loose when unloaded, and is the better knot if the sizes of the two ropes are markedly different. These bends are related to the bowline (pp. 36–7) and the double bowline (pp. 37–8). The knot is used to join in new threads for weaving and knitting, and for making and repairing nets.

This must be the thicker rope if diameters differ.

1 If the ropes are of different thicknesses, take the thicker one and form a bight with the working end on top. Pass the working end of the second rope up through the bight.

2 Lead the working end of the second rope up, then down underneath the bight, and to the front.

3 Now pass the working end under itself so that it lies across both strands of the bight.

DOUBLE SHEET BEND

5 To tie a double sheet bend, complete the sheet bend to the end of Step 3, but do not tighten. Continue the working end around the bight again and to the front.

Both working ends finish on the same side of the knot.

4 Firm the knot by pulling on the bight with one hand, and the standing part of the second rope with the other. The working ends must not finish on opposite sides of the knot.

6 Tuck the end under its own standing part and over both strands of the bight to exit. Again, the working ends must finish on the same side of the knot.

WHAT'S IT FOR? Pulling a large rope along a dock; hoisting a rope up a cliff face or across a roof

ONE-WAY SHEET BEND

Also known as a tucked sheet bend, this is a method of joining two ropes to be pulled across a surface. The one-way sheet bend is a more secure version of the sheet bend (pp. 62–3) when the rope is to be pulled across a rough surface, through water or vegetation, or over obstructions or edges, such as a house roof gutter. However, the rope must be pulled in the correct direction, not the other way, or back and forth.

2 Lead the right working end down across the front of the knot. Tuck it right to left, under the lower edge of its previous turn.

1 Complete Steps 1–3 of the sheet bend (pp. 62–3). Leave the knot loose.

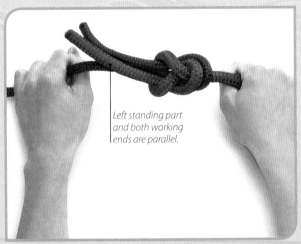

Left standing part and both working ends are parallel.

3 Tighten by pulling on both standing parts. The knot can be pulled, from left to right only, across rough surfaces and over obstructions without the ends catching.

BENDS

RIGGER'S BEND

The rigger's bend, also known as the Hunter's bend, is ideal for tying both rope and shock cord, and for joining rope to shock cord. It works well in slippery rope and will also hold in fishing line once the knot is pulled very tight. As with most bends, it is best not to leave the working ends too short. Like Ashley's bend (pp. 60–1), the knot can provide four stable, usable ends. Some will find the rigger's bend quicker and easier to tie in the hand than Ashley's bend, or at least easier to get started.

BENDS

1 Lead the ropes from opposite directions, overlap them about 18 inches (46 cm), and create a turn, with the ropes exiting to the right lying under the ropes going left.

BENDS

The rope pair should be flat and parallel, the lower rope on the outside of the turn, and the upper rope inside.

2 Take the left working end—the one belonging to the right-hand rope—and lead it through the turn from back to front. Hold it on the inner left-hand edge of the turn.

4 Pull the working ends completely through, then pull firmly on the standing parts to tighten. Make sure the working ends protrude from the knot at least a hand's width.

3 Take the right working end and lead it through the turn from front to back.

5 The knot will capsize and the two working ends will exit in opposite directions. If four usable ends are required, tie the knot near the center of the two ropes.

HITCHES

Hitches attach load-bearing cordage to spars, piles, anchors, bollards, fish hooks, trailer tie-down points, and many other objects. The choice of hitch is important if it needs to remain secure when subjected to shaking or flogging, or if the load is not constant. The angle at which the load can be applied to some hitches is also important, as is the end or ends that can be loaded. Despite their names, the anchor bend (pp. 76–7) and the topsail halyard bend (p. 85) are both hitches.

COW HITCH
- ◆ PEDIGREE COW HITCH
- ◆ COW HITCH AND TOGGLE

The cow hitch, also called a lark's head, provides a very simple method of attaching a ring or small object to a rope. It is especially useful for connecting rope items that have closed loops to keys, zipper tags, and other closed-eye fittings. The strain should be applied evenly to both ends of the rope. If you wish to finish with just one standing part, tie the pedigree cow hitch. The pedigree cow hitch will hold in fishing line and shock cord.

Widen the bight and fold it back over and around the ring so that the bight lies on its own standing part. Pull on the ring and standing parts to tighten.

Form a bight and pass it through the ring, from front to back. The ring must be able to pass through the bight.

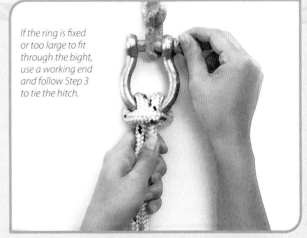

If the ring is fixed or too large to fit through the bight, use a working end and follow Step 3 to tie the hitch.

Pass the end through the ring, front to back, left and to the front, cross over the standing part, make another turn around the ring, back to front, and under the crossing.

HITCHES

PEDIGREE COW HITCH

Feed working end into the hitch from its own side

4 Repeat Steps 1 and 2, but before tightening, lead the working end away from the hitch then back under its own turn and that of the standing part. Pull through firmly.

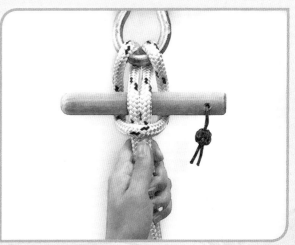

6 After inserting the toggle, pull on the standing parts to tighten. The load must be taken by both standing parts.

COW HITCH & TOGGLE

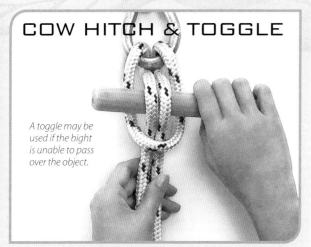

A toggle may be used if the bight is unable to pass over the object.

5 Lead the bight through the ring and bring it down over its standing part. Draw the standing ends partly into the bight, and insert the toggle .

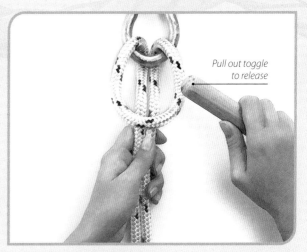

Pull out toggle to release

7 To release, pull out the toggle. A toggle is simply an item of convenient length that is strong enough to take the strain. The greater the load, the tighter the toggle will be held.

HITCHES

HITCHES

PILE HITCH
• DOUBLE PILE HITCH

Pile hitches can be used for attaching a dinghy to a post, or pile, or an anchor line to a bollard. They can be tied in the bight—requiring no access to the ends of the rope—or at the end of a rope. The length of the working end required to tie the hitch will depend on the diameter of the post. To untie, ease some of the working end back into the hitch until there is enough slack to lift the bight off the top of the post. The double pile hitch is very secure but a little more complicated to untie.

1 Form a bight long enough to pass several times around the post. Hold the standing parts in one hand. With the other, lead the bight around the post, under both standing parts.

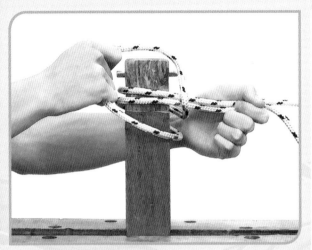

Widen the bight and place it over the top of the post.

DOUBLE PILE HITCH

Complete Step 1, then wind the bight around the post a second time before placing it over the post. The second winding is made lower down the post than the first.

Pull evenly on both ends to firm the hitch. If the rope is sticking and not tightening evenly around the post, you may have to help it, but be careful not to catch your fingers.

Adjust the hitch as for Step 3. With both hitches, make sure that you hold the ends together until the bight is placed over the post, so that both ends are captured.

CLOVE HITCH

• CLOVE HITCH: ALTERNATE

The clove hitch is a quick and easily remembered knot for attaching a rope to a pole, but it can slip on a smooth surface. The load can be applied to either end of the rope. Steps 1 and 2 show the clove hitch tied with a working end. The alternate "in-the-hand" method shown in Steps 3–6 allows the hitch to be readily tied in the bight—anywhere along the rope. This method can be used where you can slip the hitch over the end of a pole.

HITCHES

1 Lead the working end over and down behind the pole, then up in front and over itself to the left.

2 Lead the working end diagonally across the turn, around the back of the rail again, then upward under itself. You have formed two half hitches. Pull the ends to tighten.

CLOVE HITCH: ALTERNATE

Two similarly sized overhand turns

Direction the loops will move in Step 4

3 If you don't have easy access to the ends of the rope, tie the clove hitch using this alternate method. Begin by making two consecutive overhand turns.

5 When viewed from the side, the two half hitches can be identified. It is the same knot as shown in Step 2.

Left turn sitting over right

4 Slide the left-hand turn over the right, then slide the fingers of the left hand through the center of both loops.

6 Simply slide the half hitches over the end of the pole and tighten.

HITCHES

MARLINSPIKE HITCH

The marlinspike hitch can be used to temporarily secure a tool or to make a handle in thin cord to provide better grip. It was often tied around a marlinspike, which gave the knot its name, but may be tied around tool handles for hoisting up a tree or onto a roof. If there is no spike available, a pencil makes a good substitute. Before starting this method, tie off the standing part so that you can apply tension to the cord.

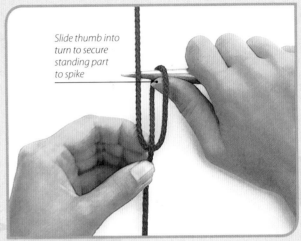

Slide thumb into turn to secure standing part to spike

2 Leaving the spike inside the turn, raise it, taking the loose portion of the turn with it, and slide the spike behind the standing part. The right thumb passes into the turn.

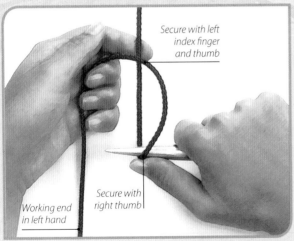

Secure with left index finger and thumb

Working end in left hand

Secure with right thumb

1 With the spike in your right hand, hold it against the cord with your thumb. Raise the working part above the spike, make an overhand turn, and secure the intersection.

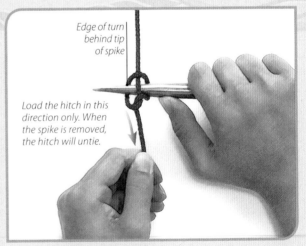

Edge of turn behind tip of spike

Load the hitch in this direction only. When the spike is removed, the hitch will untie.

3 With the left fingers, pick up the forward edge of the turn, take it left, over the standing part and slip it behind the tip of the spike. Pull down with the spike to apply tension.

BARREL HITCH

The barrel hitch is a quick and simple method of securing a barrel for hoisting upright. The same hitch can be tied around a box. Be careful that the rope is positioned under the center of the barrel, and that the upper hitches are located opposite each other, and well above the barrel's center of gravity. You will need a length of rope about three times the maximum circumference of the barrel.

Separate overhand knot into two hitches

2 Separate the overhand knot at its midpoint so that you have two opposing hitches. Maneuver the halves around opposite sides of the barrel.

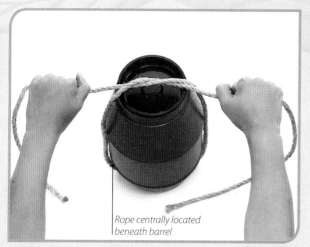

Rope centrally located beneath barrel

1 Slip the midpoint of the rope beneath the center of the barrel. Lead the ends up opposite sides of the barrel and tie a loose overhand knot (p. 17) at the top.

Tie the ends with a fisherman's knot (p. 56).

3 Ensure the rope is located correctly beneath the barrel and that the hitches are central and opposing. Maintain upward tension and tie the ends together to form a sling.

ANCHOR BEND

• ROUND TURN AND
TWO HALF HITCHES

The anchor bend, also known as the fisherman's bend, is a quite secure knot but, perhaps because it looks so simple, is most often completed by the addition of a half hitch. It will hold in shock cord, however the extra half hitch is of no benefit. The round turn and two half hitches is particularly simple to tie, but it will not hold at all in shock cord.

1 Make a round turn through a ring, winding from back to front and left to right. Do not pull the turn tight yet, as the working end needs to pass through it first.

2 Lead the working end left behind the standing part, then to the front, and tuck it to the right beneath both windings of the round turn.

Pull on both the standing part and working end to tighten the knot around the ring. This is a completed anchor bend, but a half hitch is usually added.

Pull tight

ROUND TURN AND TWO HALF HITCHES

Round turn

First half hitch

Make a round turn through the ring as in Step 1. Pass the working end around behind the standing part, to the front, and under itself, to make the first half hitch. Pull tight.

With half hitch added

Pull tight

Pass the working end around behind the standing part again, to the front, and under itself. Pull the working end as tight as possible.

Pull each half hitch very tight

Second half hitch added

Continue the working end in the same direction, around behind the standing part and to the front again, and make the second half hitch. Pull very tight.

HITCHES

PRUSIK KNOT

The Prusik knot, also known as the Prusik hitch, is excellent for attaching a loop of light line to a taut length of rope. Without load, the Prusik knot will release its grip and can be repositioned easily on the rope. Tighten the windings and apply load at right angles—that is, in the same direction as the rope—and it will grip once more. The strain must be applied evenly to both ends of the line, so tying them into a loop is ideal. To grip well, the line should be no more than half the diameter of the rope.

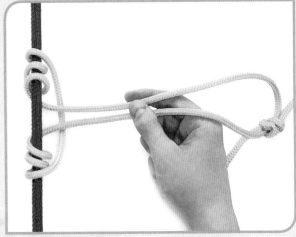

2 Open out the bight of the cow hitch. Wind the knotted end neatly around the rope and under the bight three or four times, so that each turn is inside the other.

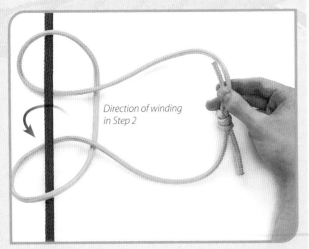

Direction of winding in Step 2

1 Take a length of line about 3 feet (1 m) long and tie the ends together with a fisherman's knot (p. 56). Form a loose cow hitch (p. 68) around the fixed, taut rope.

Windings must not overlap. Friction will prevent the knot from sliding.

3 Ease the two sets of windings together. Rotate the windings around the rope with your fingers to work the slack out of the bight and into the knotted loop end.

BUNTLINE HITCH

This hitch's name is from its use on square-rigged vessels, where it secures buntlines to the foot of a square sail. Although used as a hitch, the knot is actually a sliding loop. It is considered secure, no matter how much a sail flogs, or flaps, in the wind. When pulled very tight, it may need a marlinspike to help untie it. One solution is to tie a slipped buntline hitch by making the final diagonal tuck in Step 3 with a bight, so that a tug on the working end will release the knot, but this will not suit all applications.

2 Wind around behind the standing part and to the front, then cross diagonally left over the turn.

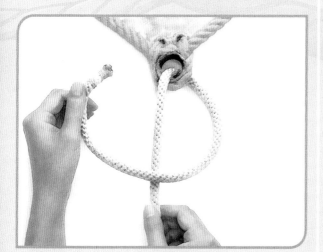

1 Lead the working end of the rope through the ring, from front to back and left to right, then back across to the left to make an overhand turn.

Two half hitches secure the working end to the standing part.

3 Continue around behind the standing part of the turn, then tuck left beneath itself. Tighten and slide the knot to the ring.

HITCHES

HIGHWAYMAN'S HITCH

While the name may conjure up visions of robbers in the Wild West tying their horses to a hitching rail, ready for a fast get-away, there is no evidence of this hitch's use in such criminal activity. It is a good knot to know because of the way it instantly releases with a tug on the working end. However, it is not the most secure of hitches: constant movement of the standing part, or the application and release of tension, can easily loosen it.

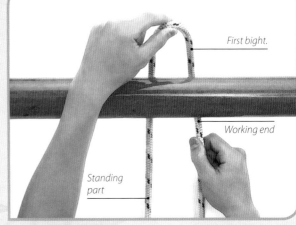

First bight.

Working end

Standing part

1 Form a long bight in the left hand, with the working end to the right of the standing part, and lead it up behind the rail. Leave a longish working end.

Second bight

2 With the right hand, form a second bight in the standing part, with the remainder of the standing part on the right side of this new bight.

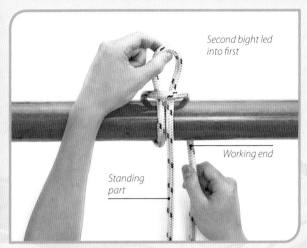

Second bight led into first

Working end

Standing part

Tuck this second bight up through the first, hold it in place with your left hand, and tighten the first bight around the second by pulling on the working end.

Third bight led into second

Lead this third bight fully up into the second, so that there is no slack around the rail.

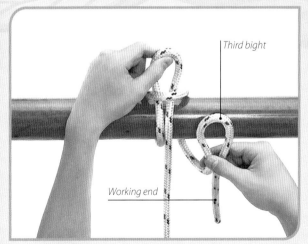

Third bight

Working end

With the right hand, form a third bight in the working part, with the working end to the right.

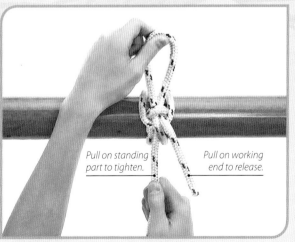

Pull on standing part to tighten.

Pull on working end to release.

Pull on the standing part to firm the second bight around the third. To release, pull on the working end and the hitch will slide apart.

TIMBER HITCH

• KILLICK HITCH

The timber hitch is an easy method of securing a rope to a pole, and it requires only a single passing around it, which is an advantage if the pole is heavy. With the timber hitch tied at the center of gravity, the pole can be hoisted. The addition of a half hitch forms the killick hitch, which allows the pole to be towed, on land or through water, with directional stability. The timber hitch is also used to attach nylon strings to a guitar bridge.

HITCHES

Use more windings for bigger, heavier poles.

Wind the working end around the turn again once, twice, or three times. Pull tight on the standing part and ease the slack out of the windings through the working end.

Alternatively, go over the turn first, then under it from left to right

Make a loose turn around the pole from the back to the front. Pass the working end behind the standing part, to the front, and under the turn.

KILLICK HITCH

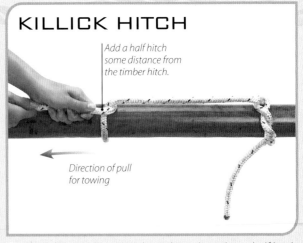

Add a half hitch some distance from the timber hitch.

Direction of pull for towing

Lead the standing part along the pole and tie a half hitch (p. 6). Tying it nearer the end provides better stability when towing, but too near the end and it will slip off.

ROLLING HITCH
•TAUTLINE HITCH

The rolling hitch is used to tie a rope to a pole or to larger rope, when the load is to be applied, at an angle between 45 and 90 degrees to the pole. The direction of the load, or strain, will dictate the way in which the knot must be tied. The hitches shown here take the strain from the right. To take a load from the left, the hitch can be tied as a mirror image, or tied the same way but from the other side of the pole. The tautline hitch works similarly, and is suitable for attaching a line to a taut rope.

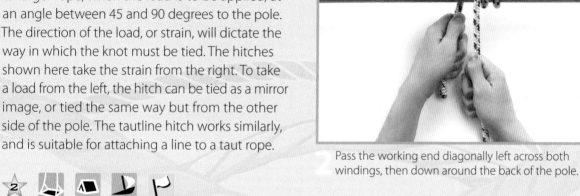

Pass the working end diagonally left across both windings, then down around the back of the pole.

HITCHES

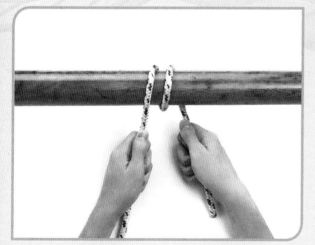

Begin the hitch with a round turn, proceeding up and over, and from left to right.

Tuck the working end up under the diagonal. Note that the rolling hitch is actually a clove hitch (p. 72) with an extra turn around the pole on the right.

Load the hitch from the right.

4 Pull both ends to tighten. The load can be applied from the right of the hitch. For loading from the left, begin tying the hitch as in Step 1, but winding from right to left.

6 Lead the working end up behind the rope, to the front, and tuck it under itself, parallel to the standing part. The knot looks like a cow hitch (p. 68) with an extra turn.

TAUTLINE HITCH

5 Tie this hitch in line that is half the diameter of the taut rope, or thinner. Complete Step 1 of the rolling hitch, then lead the working end left in front of the standing part.

Load the hitch from the right.

To apply strain at an angle less than 45 degrees to the rope, consider using a Prusik knot (p. 78), but note that both ends of the line must be equally loaded.

7 Pull both ends to firm the hitch tight around the rope. As with the rolling hitch, the strain can be applied from the direction in which the initial overhand turn was made.

TOPSAIL HALYARD BEND

The topsail halyard bend is ideal for tying a halyard to a spar, or a rope to a pole, so that it can be hoisted. Unlike a clove hitch (p. 72) or a rolling hitch (p. 83), where the strain tends to rotate the pole, the topsail halyard bend naturally accepts the load at the pole's center. It is a very strong and ingenious knot that has the added advantage of spreading the load evenly across the width of three windings, lessening the compression that would occur with a clove hitch.

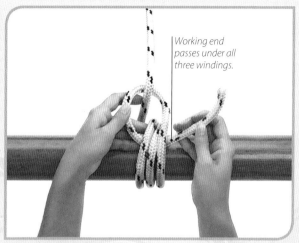

Working end passes under all three windings.

Bring the working end to the front and tuck it under all three windings. The turns must be loose—too tight and it will be difficult to lead the working end under.

Working end behind standing part

Leading from above, make a round turn around the pole, from back to front and left to right. Add a single turn to form three windings. Lead the rope diagonally left and behind.

Working end passes over two windings, then under one.

Reverse direction and lead the working end right to left, over the top of the first two windings, then under the third. Tighten from the standing part to the working end.

HITCHES

PALOMAR KNOT

The palomar knot is a simple method for attaching fishing line to a hook, ring, or swivel. It is quick to tie and very strong, but not as resistant to abrasion as snelling (pp. 88–9). When attaching line to a hook, it is best to pass the bight through the eye from the tip to the back of the shank, especially where the eye is angled toward the back. This adds to the directional stability of the hook. Some argue that it makes the hook less likely to catch a fish; others counter that the hooked fish is less likely to get away.

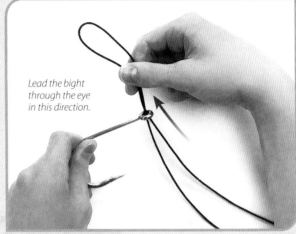

Lead the bight through the eye in this direction.

1 Form a bight slightly longer than the length of the hook. Pass the bight through the eye, from the tip of the hook to the back of the shank.

HITCHES

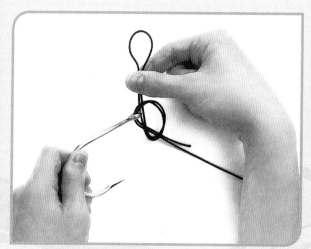

2 Using the bight as the working end, tie an overhand knot (p. 17) around the eye, making sure that the end of the line, the "tail," remains captive.

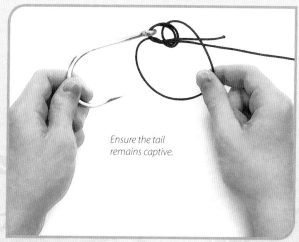

Ensure the tail remains captive.

4 With the hook passed completely through the bight, pull on the standing part and the working end to make the bight firm against the overhand knot.

Open up the bight and pass it around the hook.

3 Pull enough slack out of the overhand knot so that the bight can be passed over the end of the hook.

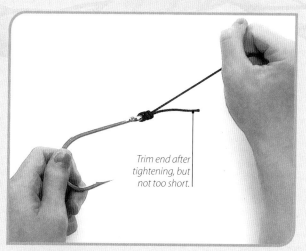

Trim end after tightening, but not too short.

5 In stiffer, heavy breaking strain line, it can be difficult to firm up the knot. Wetting the line helps, but tends to make it more slippery in your fingers.

HITCHES

SNELLING A HOOK

Snelling was the only method of binding a line to a hook in the days when hooks had a flattened spade, rather than an eye, at the end of the shank. This snelling method is a little more awkward than the palomar knot (pp. 86–7), but is less affected by abrasion and less likely to be bitten through by a fish. Other methods of snelling a hook tend to be more complicated. When fishing line is either very fine or very stiff, keeping bights and windings under control while tying can be difficult.

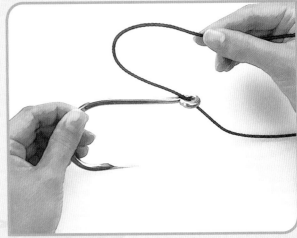

1 Pass the line through the eye in a direction from the tip of the hook to the back of the shank. Leave a working end about four times the length of the hook.

HITCHES

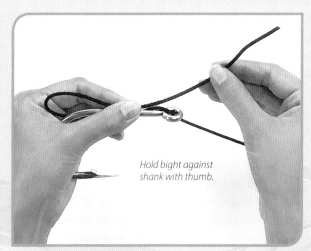

Hold bight against shank with thumb.

2 Lead the working end down the length of the shank, then back toward the eye, making a bight almost the length of the shank.

4 Lead the working end upward through the remaining portion of the bight. Pull hard to make sure that the windings are tight.

Wind tightly down the shank.

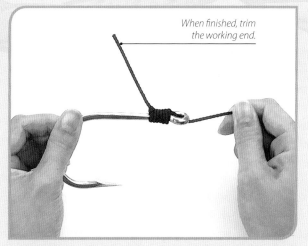

When finished, trim the working end.

3 Hold the bight firmly against the shank. Beginning just below the eye, wind the working end around the shank and bight four or five times, or up to six times for a large hook.

5 Tug hard on the standing part to pull the bight tight around the working end and slide the knot up to the eye.

HITCHES

HITCHES

TRUCKER'S HITCH

The trucker's hitch is also known as the waggoner's hitch and dolly knot. As it can be tensioned further after tightening, it is suitable for tying tent stays, or securing a load on a trailer. The hitch provides leverage, allowing the rope to be pulled tight, and uses up any excess cordage. It requires a length of rope four to five times the distance from the hitch's starting point to the securing point. The trucker's hitch is only stable under tension, so make sure that there is no chance of the load shifting.

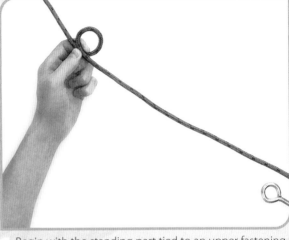

1 Begin with the standing part tied to an upper fastening point. Rotating counterclockwise, make a small overhand turn and secure it in your left hand.

2 With your right hand, form a bight in the working part. It will need to have a length approximately half the distance from the turn to the securing point.

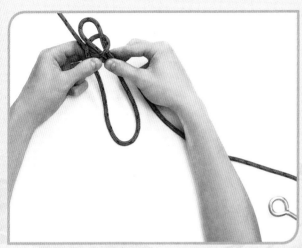

Lead the end of the bight into the overhand turn from below—not too far in, about a fifth of its length will do. Secure the bight and overhand turn in your left hand.

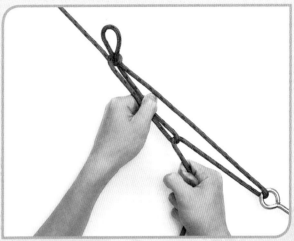

Lead the working end up through the shank from back to front. Apply downward tension to the working end. The turn will grip the bight and you can let go with the left hand.

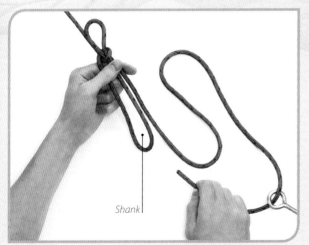

Shank

This forms a new, lower bight, called a shank. Lead the working end down and through the lower fastening point.

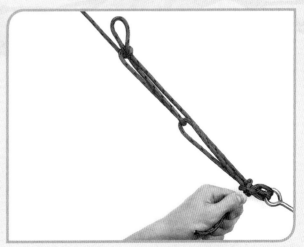

Pull the end as tight as necessary and tie it off above the fastening point—a couple of half hitches (p. 6) should do. The trucker's hitch requires some practice to master.

LASHINGS

Lashing is a method of fastening structural items together with cordage. When building a tree house, for example, use lashings to secure the beams, cross bracing, and supports. While bindings are temporary fastenings, and use just one or two turns of cordage, lashings are more permanent and use multiple windings. The cordage acts as a clamping mechanism, but also provides friction to help prevent the lashed items slipping against one another. Some lashings work best in cordage with some stretch.

SQUARE LASHING

Square lashing is a relatively easy way to secure two poles at right angles. It is stronger and more permanent than the transom knot (p. 32) but takes more time and cordage. Be careful with the tension and the number of windings: the lashing must be strong enough for the job, but not so tight that the poles are bent. The lashing can also begin with a timber hitch (p. 82), constrictor knot (pp. 28–9), or multiple overhand knot (pp. 17–18). Experiment to find out which works best.

LASHINGS

Later additional windings will lock the tail securely.

Tie a clove hitch (p. 72) to the vertical pole. Wind the tail and standing part together. Place the horizontal pole on top of the vertical. Lead the ends over both poles to the right.

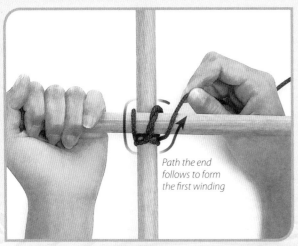

Path the end follows to form the first winding

Maintaining the tension, lead the cord behind the upper vertical pole, over and down in front of the left horizontal pole, around behind the lower vertical and to the front.

Frapping turns do not bind pole to pole but compress the existing windings.

Commence the frapping turns. Make a turn over the right horizontal, then wind clockwise between the two poles three or four times.

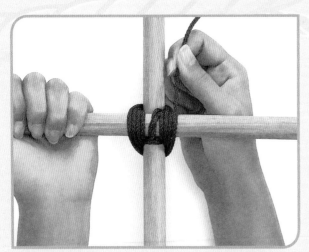

Repeat the winding process about four times. The number of windings will depend on the diameter of the poles and the thickness of the cord.

Clove hitch to finish

Stop at the top left and tie a tight clove hitch (p. 72) around the upper vertical, so the lashing can't slide or rotate under tension.

DIAGONAL LASHING

Diagonal lashing is used to pull cross-bracing poles together. The two poles don't have to be at right angles. The timber hitch (p. 82) at the start pulls both poles together without changing their relative position. However, if the poles are not already fixed by some other means, the angle can be difficult to maintain during lashing. The tension applied in the diagonal lashing process isn't as great as in square lashing (pp. 93–4), but there is less chance of the poles sliding.

Lead the cord away from you and around the back

Tie a timber hitch (p. 82) around both poles, at the intersection with the widest angle. Tighten the hitch and lead the cord away from you, around the back of both poles.

LASHINGS

Commence lashing through the wider angle first.

Wind tightly over the top of the hitch and around the intersection four or five times. Unless the poles are fixed, the tighter you wind, the wider the angle becomes.

Three or four frapping turns should do.

Wind the cord counterclockwise by passing in front of the upper vertical pole, behind the left cross pole, in front of the lower vertical and behind the right cross pole.

If the poles are fixed, wind the same number of times as for the wider angle.

Now wind across the narrower intersecting angle. If the poles are not fixed, apply pressure and continue winding until you achieve the angle you want.

Tie off with a clove hitch.

Finish with a clove hitch (p. 72) around one of the poles. Align it with the end of the frapping turns so that there is little chance of the hitch sliding or rotating under tension.

SHEER LASHING

The sheer lashing can secure two poles longitudinally to reinforce or extend a pole, with one lashing at either end of the pair or at the overlap between them. Tied a little more loosely, it makes an A-frame lashing where the two poles are separated slightly and intersect at a narrow angle to form a support. The A-frame is also known as sheer legs. For an angle of more than 25 degrees, the diagonal lashing (pp. 95–6) may be a better choice.

To make an A-frame, begin the lashing far enough away from the pole ends, so that the top of the frame is deep enough for the object it will support.

Lay two poles side by side and tie together with a clove hitch (p. 72). Leave the shorter end long enough to be secured underneath the windings.

Cover the short end of the clove hitch with the lashing.

Begin winding, but not as tightly for an A-frame as for securing two poles. As a rule of thumb, make the binding length no less than the width of the two poles.

LASHINGS

Make at least two frapping turns; there is unlikely to be room for more than three.

For the frapping turns, lead the cord behind the top pole and to the front between the poles. Wind across the existing windings, between the poles.

If tying poles together to reinforce or extend them, make a tighter binding, omit the frapping turns, and finish with a clove hitch around both poles.

Finish at the opposite end to the original clove hitch and tie another clove hitch (p. 72) around one pole, not both. The hitch must be tight, and snug against the lashing.

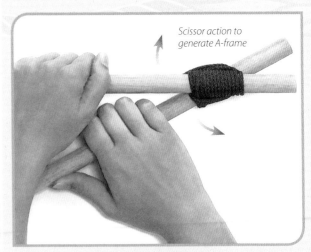

Scissor action to generate A-frame

To use as an A-frame, separate the poles by using a scissor action, stretching the cord equally at both ends of the lashing. Practice will help you apply the right lashing tension.

TRIPOD LASHING

There are different methods of tying tripod lashings but this one can be tied into a frame, transported to a site, and erected. After use it can be folded flat and taken elsewhere, with a temporary binding such as the pole lashing (pp. 24–5) securing the other end. However, it doesn't form the perfect shape of an equilateral triangle at its base. Like the sheer lashing (pp. 97–8), the angle at which the legs can be separated is determined by the length and tension of the lashing and the stretch in the cord.

Wind the short clove hitch end around the working end and lead both ends toward you across the three poles. This will help lock the clove hitch and its tail.

When beginning, allow for the width of the lashing and space to hang an item.

Lay three poles side by side, making sure the ends that will stand on the ground are even. Tie a clove hitch (p. 72) around the top pole at a suitable distance from the ends.

Start winding between the poles: under the bottom pole, over the center, under the top, then around and over, this time under the center pole, and over the bottom.

LASHINGS

Wind for about the width of two poles. Stop with the cord coming from behind the top pole. Begin frapping turns.

Begin frapping turns by leading the cord down in front of the top pole, then to the back between the top and center poles. Form two or three turns around the windings.

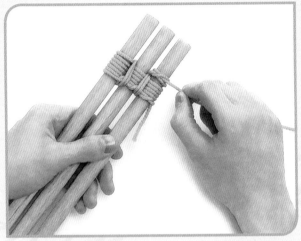

To finish, tie off with a clove hitch (p. 72) around the bottom pole. The frapping turn must lead straight into the hitch so that there is no chance of it rotating.

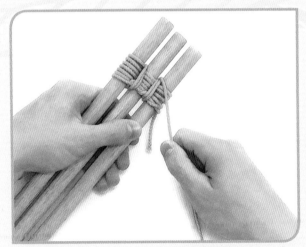

Lead the cord behind the center pole, and to the front between the center and bottom poles. Make a second set of frapping turns in the opposite direction to the first.

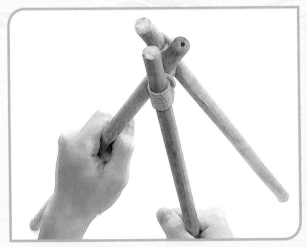

To erect the tripod, separate the outer poles and use a scissor action to swing the center pole in the opposite direction. This may be difficult if the lashing is too tight.

SPLICES

Splicing is a traditional method used to permanently join two laid ropes, add a branch rope to create a Y-join, or form an eye in the end of a rope. The splicing methods described in this book will enable you to complete all of these tasks. The eye splice (pp. 102–3) and short splice (pp. 104–5) are not difficult, however, they require a methodical approach and practice.

EYE SPLICE

An eye splice isn't actually a knot, but a means of forming an eye in the end of a length of laid rope. The method can also join a secondary piece of rope to the first to create a Y-piece, as long as the strain on each arm of the Y will be in a similar direction. A splice is used where a rope is fixed permanently to an item or slipped over a hook, pile, or bollard. Most laid ropes are Z-laid, meaning that the strands are wound clockwise, and these instructions are for Z-laid rope.

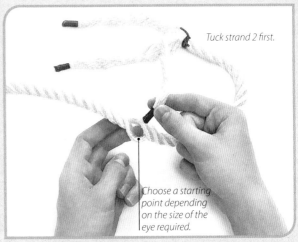

Tuck strand 2 first.

Choose a starting point depending on the size of the eye required.

2 Open the lay of the rope to raise one strand. Feed the central strand 2 diagonally left under the raised strand in the standing part. Do not pull it through completely yet.

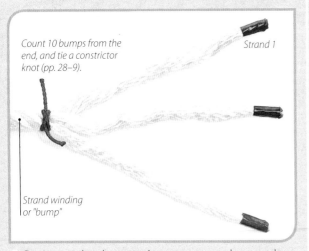

Count 10 bumps from the end, and tie a constrictor knot (pp. 28–9).

Strand 1

Strand winding or "bump"

1 Begin to unlay the rope. As you separate the strands, bind them with tape. Continue to unlay the strands up to the knot. Allocate each strand a number.

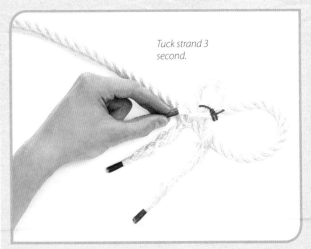

Tuck strand 3 second.

3 Feed strand 3, which is to the right of strand 2, under its corresponding right strand in the standing part, that is, the strand to the right of the one that strand 2 is tucked under.

SPLICES

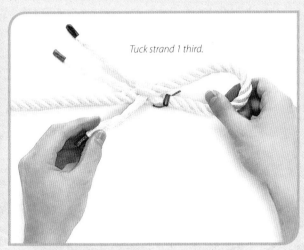

Tuck strand 1 third.

4 Rotate the rope slightly, and tuck the remaining strand 1 under its corresponding left strand of the standing part. Pull the three unlaid strands snugly up to the standing part.

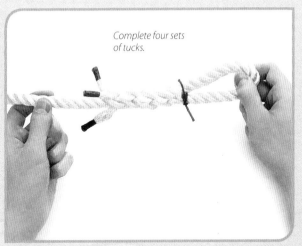

Complete four sets of tucks.

6 Maintain the even twist in the unlaid strands as you tuck. If you don't open the lay in the standing part sufficiently, the twist in the strands will increase as you go.

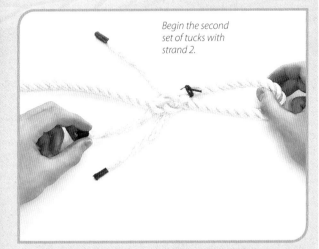

Begin the second set of tucks with strand 2.

5 Continue weaving the unlaid strands in this diagonal pattern until you have completed four sets of tucks. Three may be enough, but not if the lay of the rope is loose.

Trim and seal ends.

7 Thick rope may need the assistance of a fid for opening the lay. After the fourth tuck, the ends can be trimmed and either whipped (pp. 12–13) or heat sealed (p. 11).

SPLICES

SHORT SPLICE

This is a method of permanently joining two lengths of laid rope. It is not essential that the ropes be of exactly the same diameter, but they must be similar. When two ropes are joined with a bend, the knot will not pass over a pulley or through a block, but with the splice, as long as it is tapered and the rope size is comfortable in the sheave, it should fit through. There are other ways of joining two ropes that give a more slender result, but they are not as strong.

SPLICES

Begin tucking the left rope into the right.

2 Following the same procedure as for Steps 2–4 of the eye splice (pp. 102–3), begin to weave the left rope into the right. Make two sets of tucks.

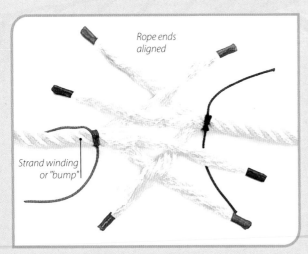

Rope ends aligned

Strand winding or "bump"

1 Tie a constrictor knot (pp. 28–9) around each piece of rope about 12 bumps from the end. Tape and number the strands and unwind them. Align the strands of the rope ends.

Two sets of tucks, left into right, completed

3 Make a set of tucks of the right rope into the left. Tighten the strands and adjust the alignment of one rope to the other. Loosen the constrictor knots as required.

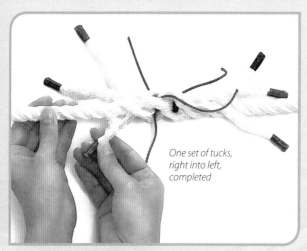

One set of tucks, right into left, completed

4 Make another set of tucks with the right rope into the left, so that there are two sets in each direction. Then make alternate sets until you have four in each direction.

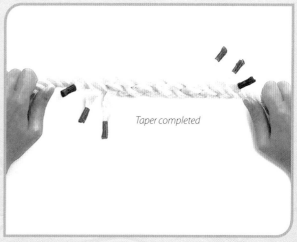

Taper completed

6 An easy way to taper is to not tuck one strand of each set after three tucks, leave out a second strand after the fourth tuck, and make a fifth tuck with the one remaining strand.

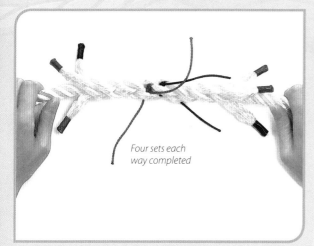

Four sets each way completed

5 The splice is completed and the ends can be trimmed and sealed. However, if you wish to taper the splice, proceed to Step 6.

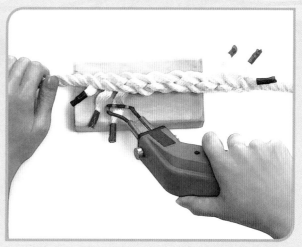

7 When the tucking of each strand is completed in the correct order, the splice will have an even and attractive taper. Trim and seal the ends neatly.

SPLICES

TRICKS

Rope tricks encompass seemingly impossible means of tying or untying a knot. They include manipulating a rope to enable a knot to be released, transferring a knot from one portion of a rope to another, and quickly turning one knot into a different one. Tricks in which apparently complicated knots are instantly untied either involve one or more slip knots, or incorporate an untying process that has the appearance of further complicating an already recognizable knot.

IMPOSSIBLE KNOT

Put a length of rope in front of your friends and challenge them to pick it up and tie a knot without letting go with either hand. The result must be a proper knot that does not collapse when the rope is pulled tight. Any kind of cordage will do, but a piece of rope will be easier to handle than thin cord. The rope or cord should be about 3 feet (1 m) long so you can comfortably demonstrate how the trick is done after everyone else has given up.

2 Keeping a firm hold on the rope, uncross your arms and move your hands apart, letting the rope slip over your wrists and hands as you do so.

1 Lay the rope on a table. Before picking it up, cross your arms over each other. Now lean over and pick up one end of the rope in each hand.

3 With this trick, you tie an overhand knot in the rope without letting go of either end.

TRICKS

HANDCUFFS PUZZLE

You and your friend put on rope "handcuffs" with a loop knot in each end for the wrists, and the two ropes linked. The kind of knot used to make the loops is not important, but the bowline (pp. 36–7) works well. The two of you must try to separate yourselves without removing the handcuffs, untying the wrist loops, or cutting the rope. This trick uses two ropes, each at least 5 feet (1.5 m) long. Thick, soft rope is best as it will not cause any chafing.

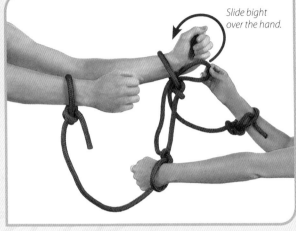

Slide bight over the hand.

2 Make a small bight in your rope and pull it toward you through your friend's wrist loop. Keep pulling until it is large enough to pass over your friend's hand.

1 Interlock the two ropes and place the handcuff loops over your own and your friend's wrists. The loops must be big enough to slide easily over the hands and onto the wrists.

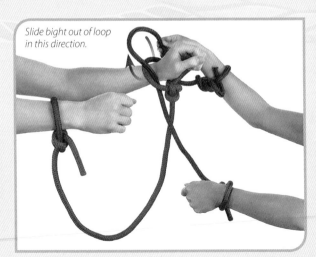

Slide bight out of loop in this direction.

3 Pass the bight over the hand from the thumb side to the little finger side. A gentle tug will pull it out of your friend's wrist loop, leaving you both free.

TRICKS

RING DROP

This trick allows you to remove an object threaded onto a loop, without letting go of the loop or breaking the object. The loop should be made from a length of thin cord about 3 feet (1 m) long and threaded through the center of a ring or bead. You can either hand the loop and threaded object to your friends and ask them to work out how to free the object without dropping the loop, or, once you have had a bit of practice, demonstrate the trick very quickly and let others try to work out how you did it.

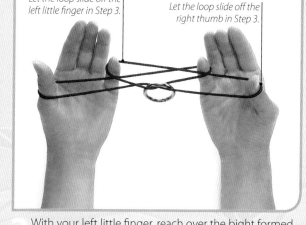

Let the loop slide off the left little finger in Step 3.

Let the loop slide off the right thumb in Step 3.

2 With your left little finger, reach over the bight formed by the right little finger, and hook it around the upper strand to the right of the ring, again from behind.

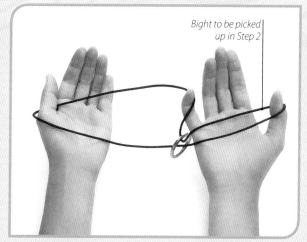

Bight to be picked up in Step 2

1 With the loop hanging over both your thumbs, hook the right little finger around the upper strand, to the left of the ring and from behind.

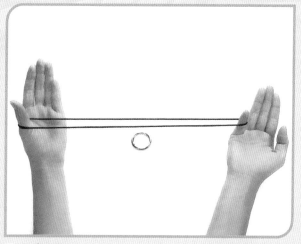

3 To free the ring, move your hands apart while letting the loop slip off the left little finger and the right thumb.

TRICKS

NOT A KNOT

This trick, which begins with a reef knot, looks very complicated but the seemingly secure knot falls apart completely when pulled tight. The final step is easiest to carry out if thin cord or flexible rope is used rather than thick or stiff rope. A piece of cord about 3 feet (1 m) long is ideal. You can either demonstrate the puzzle yourself, or give a reef knot to your friends and challenge them to make it collapse without untying it.

2 Lead the same working end through the center of the reef knot, again from back to front.

1 Form a loop and tie a reef knot (pp. 22–3). Pick up the working end that emerges toward the back of the knot and lead it through the loop from back to front.

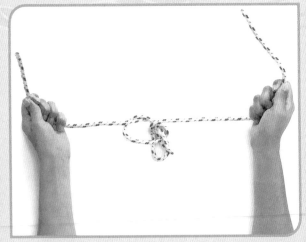

3 Pull firmly on both ends of the cord. The original reef knot will collapse and disappear completely.

TRICKS

DECORATIVE

Decorative knots are usually practical knots that are also attractive. The Turk's head has many applications, including improving grip on handrails and boat hook handles. Mats protect decks in high-wear areas or around deck fittings. Lanyards prevent small tools being dropped and lost. Sometimes a change of cordage can turn one design into a different object altogether—in thin cord, Solomon bar (pp. 133–5) can make a zipper pull, and in thick rope or old mooring line it can make a boat fender.

MONKEY'S FIST

Monkey's fists are a family of spherical knots, usually fitted with a core. The simplest is the best known. It weights one end of a heaving line for throwing between boats, and makes a good zipper, blind, or light switch pull. The monkey's fist can be used as a stopper where the knot is left permanently tied. With a hand grip made from a loop knot or an eye splice (pp. 102–3) in the short tail, it makes a dog's tug-of-war or throw toy. With a buoyant core, it keeps a key dropped overboard afloat, and hung up to swing on a boat, discourages seagulls.

Work the turns from the bottom up.

Tighten so that the turns stay in place, but not so tight that the core cannot be inserted in Step 4.

Secure the turns between your fingers and thumb. Next, make three horizontal turns by leading the working end around the outside of the original turns, coiling upward.

The number of turns determines the size of the knot. Make more turns in Steps 1–3 to achieve a larger result.

Anchor the standing end with the thumb and take three vertical turns around the hand, pulling them up snugly so they are easy to secure in the following step.

The working end should leave the knot at the top left.

Work the third set of turns away from you as well as counterclockwise.

Lead the working end inside the first set of turns, above the second. Make a third set of three turns around the outside of the second, but inside the first, working counterclockwise.

DECORATIVE

Never use heavy cores in heaving lines, as serious injury can result.

Plastic ball core

Open a gap where any two sets of turns cross each other and insert the core. Close the gap to conceal the core.

KEY FOB / ZIPPER PULL

For a key fob or zipper pull needing a loop, pick up the working end behind where the first set of turns cross it and pull the amount of slack for the loop back into the knot.

Tuck one end inside the knot. Be careful not to pull it out again when tightening the knot.

Tuck the working end inside the knot. Gradually tighten the knot with an awl, working the slack from the standing end toward the working end. Fair up the knot with a hammer.

Cow hitch the loop to a zipper or single key. Attach a split ring for a multi-key fob.

Work the slack for the loop around the knot until it is in the center of the second set of turns. Cut off the working end and tuck it inside the knot.

DECORATIVE

KRINGLE MAT

This is known as the kringle mat because the basic knot resembles the pretzel-shaped kringle symbol on traditional Danish bakery signs. It is straightforward to tie, but make sure to keep the cord free of twist and the knots evenly sized. Five interlocking knots make a piece suitable to use as a small floor mat, decorative or heat-proof table mat, or drink coaster. Mats with six or more knots have a larger center hole and can be placed or formed around a central object, such as a lamp base, or around a deck fitting as a thump mat.

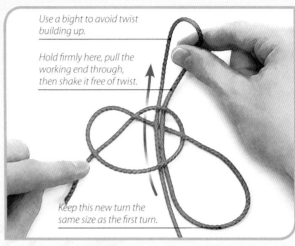

Use a bight to avoid twist building up.

Hold firmly here, pull the working end through, then shake it free of twist.

Keep this new turn the same size as the first turn.

Form a bight in the working end. Pass it under the lower strand of the first turn, over the working end that was laid across the top of it, and under the top of the turn.

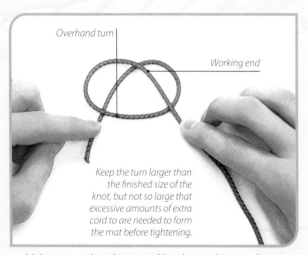

Overhand turn

Working end

Keep the turn larger than the finished size of the knot, but not so large that excessive amounts of extra cord to are needed to form the mat before tightening.

Make an overhand turn and lay the working end across the turn. If using light cord, the kringle mat can be tricky to keep in place. Try pinning the work to a cork tile.

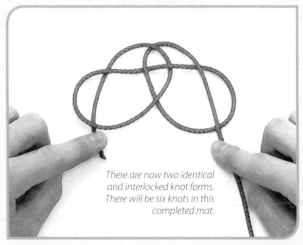

There are now two identical and interlocked knot forms. There will be six knots in this completed mat.

Lay the working end over the new overhand turn. Repeat Step 2 to tie a third knot linked with the second. Continue until the work has five knots, one short of the final number.

DECORATIVE

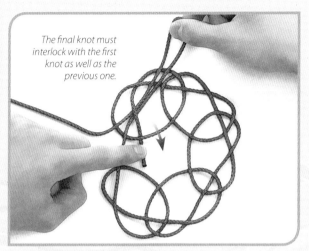

The final knot must interlock with the first knot as well as the previous one.

Lead a working-end bight over the first knot's upper strand, under the standing end, and—following the arrow—over the first knot's lower strand.

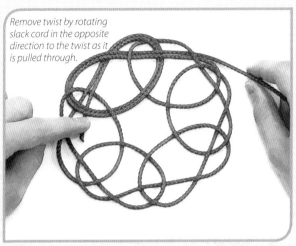

Remove twist by rotating slack cord in the opposite direction to the twist as it is pulled through.

Double the knot by following the standing part with the working end. Follow the knot around as many times as necessary, gently working the slack out of the knot.

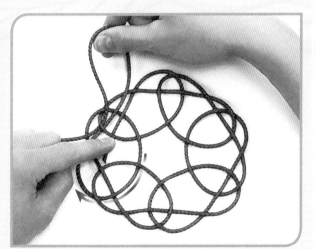

Lead a working-end bight under, over, and under, through the previous knot. Lead it over and under once more to lie next to the standing end on the outside, and pull through.

For greater stability, stitch adjacent strands together on the underside in 2–3 places.

Cut and heat-seal the ends and stitch them to the adjacent strand on the underside of the mat.

OCEAN MAT

Also known as an ocean plait mat, this oval mat is an excellent way to recycle old rope. Thicker cord is the best practice material, and finer cord may be pinned as for the kringle mat (p. 114–15). Begin with an overhand knot (p.17). Rotate it 180 degrees so that the ends are at the bottom. One end may be kept short, so that all slack is pulled out of the mat in one direction, or the cord may be middled first so that the mat is worked in both directions.

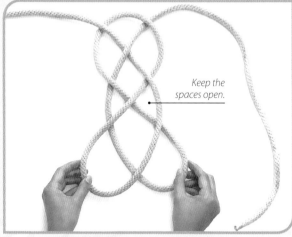

Keep the spaces open.

Lead the left-hand loop to the right and lay the right-hand loop over the top of it. Keep the spaces open as the ends will be woven through them in following steps.

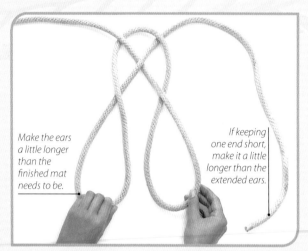

Make the ears a little longer than the finished mat needs to be.

If keeping one end short, make it a little longer than the extended ears.

Move the left-hand end upward clockwise and the right-hand end upward counterclockwise, opening two "ears" in the knot. Extend the ears and twist both clockwise.

Pick up the top right end. Lead it over the bight at the top of the long loop that now slants to the left, under both strands of the other long loop, and over once more.

DECORATIVE

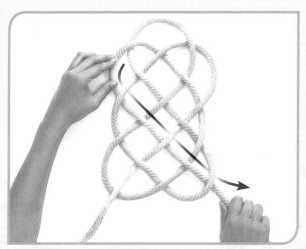

Lead the other end under, over, under, over, and under to lock the knot. Make sure that the mat shape is even, symmetrical, and slightly larger than the finished mat is to be.

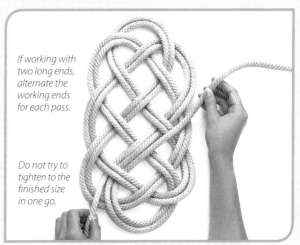

If working with two long ends, alternate the working ends for each pass.

Do not try to tighten to the finished size in one go.

Continue to follow the knot as many times as necessary to fill out the spaces. When finished, work the slack out from the standing end in two or more complete passes.

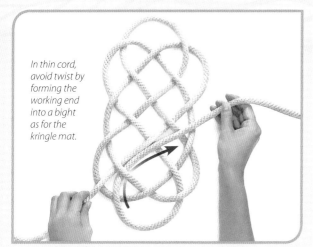

In thin cord, avoid twist by forming the working end into a bight as for the kringle mat.

The short left end becomes the standing end. Lead the working end over and under the next two bights so it is parallel to the standing end. Continue doubling the knot.

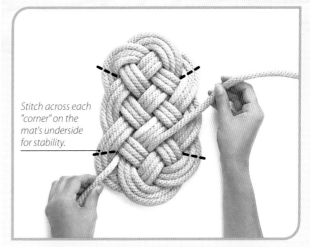

Stitch across each "corner" on the mat's underside for stability.

Cut and heat-seal the ends, and stitch or whip them on the underside. Unless the mat is small and the cord very stiff, stitch adjacent strands together on the underside.

KNIFE LANYARD KNOT

• CHINESE BUTTON

The single knife lanyard knot makes a simple zipper pull or key fob. When tightened up as the Chinese button, it makes an attractive small stopper that is traditionally used as a soft button or frog-style toggle fastening on bags and jacket fronts. The double Chinese button (pp. 121–3), double knife lanyard knot (pp. 124–5), and 4-lead, 3-bight Turk's head (pp. 127–9) are all based on this same method of tying the knife lanyard knot in the hand.

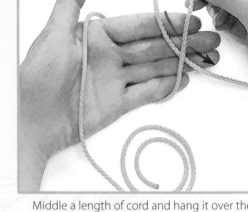

Middle a length of cord and hang it over the hand. Make an underhand turn in the end that lies across the back of the hand.

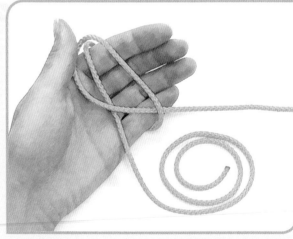

Place the turn over the cord that lies across the palm of the hand. Hold the turn in place with the thumb.

DECORATIVE

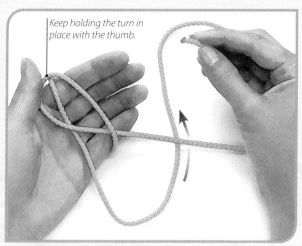

Keep holding the turn in place with the thumb.

Lead the other end behind the end leading out of the turn.

Tuck one end up through the opening in the center of the knot from underneath. This creates the Chinese button. For the knife lanyard knot, follow the arrow instead.

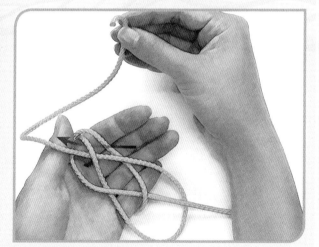

Tuck this end over the turn, under itself, and over the other side of the turn to create a carrick bend (p. 59) tied in opposite ends of the same cord.

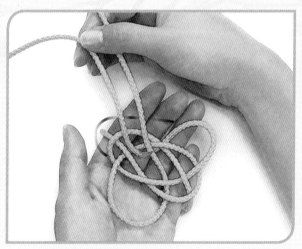

For the Chinese button, tuck the other end up through the center in the same way. For the knife lanyard knot, follow the arrow instead. Work excess slack out of the knot.

DECORATIVE

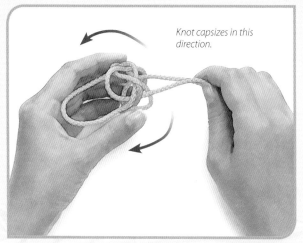

Knot capsizes in this direction.

Slide the knot off the hand, hold it loosely, and pull to the left while pulling the ends to the right. Work slack out of the knot, from the base of each side of the loop to each end.

The loop may be cow hitched onto a zipper or key.

When the knot is tight and evenly shaped, the ends can be cut off flush and fused together, left longer as a pair of tails, or unpicked with an awl to make a tassel.

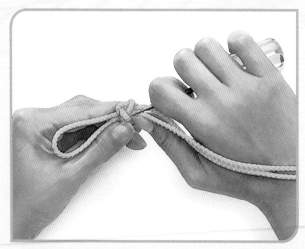

Tighten the knot with an awl, again working from the base of each side of the loop. Fair the knot into an even shape with a hammer, then tighten once more if necessary.

CHINESE BUTTON

To keep a tiny center loop, put a safety pin through it before tightening the knot to stop the small loop being pulled through by accident.

Working the loop almost out of the knife lanyard knot when tightening it produces a Chinese button. The button may also be tightened so that the loop disappears.

DECORATIVE

DOUBLE CHINESE BUTTON

The double Chinese button is used in the same way as the single—or "undoubled"—Chinese button (p. 120): as a soft button or frog-style toggle fastening on bags and jacket fronts. The double button is larger and bulkier than the single and is tied without the single button's optional small center loop.

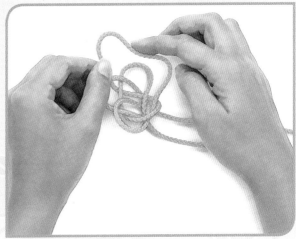

Push the center of the top loop down flat across the middle of the center opening.

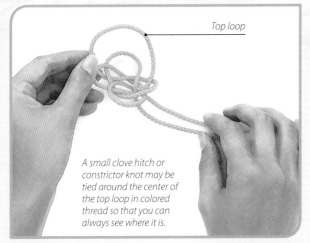

Top loop

A small clove hitch or constrictor knot may be tied around the center of the top loop in colored thread so that you can always see where it is.

Follow Steps 1–6 of the knife lanyard knot (pp. 118–19), keeping the center opening fairly large. Palm downward, slide the knot off your hand onto a work surface, top loop up.

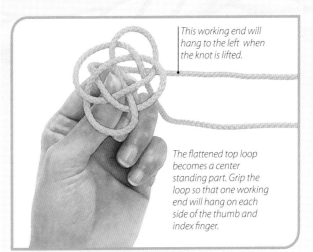

This working end will hang to the left when the knot is lifted.

The flattened top loop becomes a center standing part. Grip the loop so that one working end will hang on each side of the thumb and index finger.

Pick up the knot and hold the center of the flattened top loop firmly from underneath, taking care not to disturb the shape. Work the slack out of the knot.

DECORATIVE

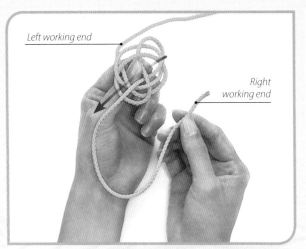

Pick up the right working end. Lead it upward to the left of the center standing part, keeping it below the thumb. Pull the slack through and let it hang over the top.

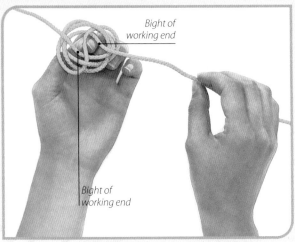

Pull the slack through once more. The bights of the working ends will be pushed together in the next step.

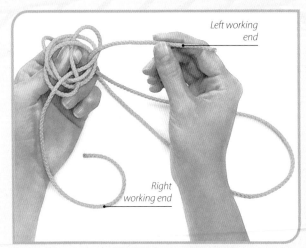

Pick up the working end that is hanging down on the left hand side. Lead it upward to the right of the center standing part, keeping it above the index finger.

Push the bights of the two working ends together and transfer your grip to these bights. Begin doubling the knot by leading each working end parallel to the other.

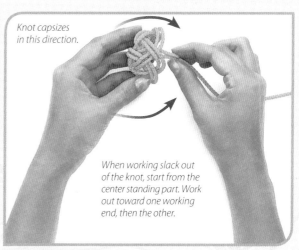

Knot capsizes in this direction.

When working slack out of the knot, start from the center standing part. Work out toward one working end, then the other.

Continue doubling the knot until the working ends lie on either side of the center standing part.

Holding both ends in the right hand, capsize the knot toward the working ends in a mushroom shape. Work the slack out of the knot with an awl.

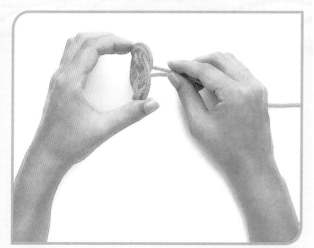

Pick up both working ends in the right hand and hold them close to the knot. Lightly hold the rim of the knot with the left hand, ready to capsize it into its final shape.

Fair the knot up into an even shape with a small hammer, then tighten once more if necessary.

Bulkier zipper pull or key fob; wrist or neck lanyard for small tools or ornaments

DOUBLE KNIFE LANYARD KNOT

• TOOL LANYARD

The double knife lanyard knot, like the single knife lanyard knot (pp. 118–20), makes a zipper pull or key fob but with a bulkier knot that is easier to grip. The larger knot also allows one working end to be fed back into the knot to create a second loop for cow hitching to a tool or ornament, such as a knife. The item can then be hung from the neck or wrist. Be careful, as this knot has no safety release catch.

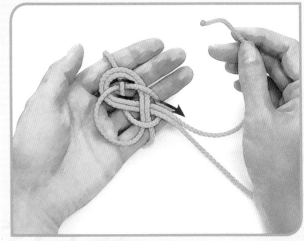

Continue following the knot with this end until it emerges from the knot parallel with the other end.

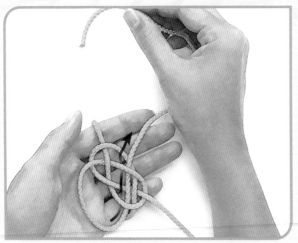

Begin with Steps 1–4 of the knife lanyard knot (pp. 118–19). Lead the left working end under the adjacent bight, over the other end, and under the next bight to form a loop.

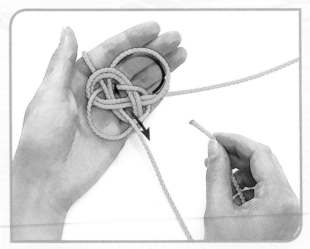

Now lead the second end over the first and under the adjacent bight to form a second side loop. Weave it through the knot parallel to the existing strands.

DECORATIVE

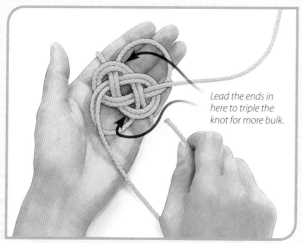

Lead the ends in here to triple the knot for more bulk.

The knot is now doubled. To triple the knot, lead each end parallel with the side loop and into the knot. Follow the knot again until each end emerges in the side loop center.

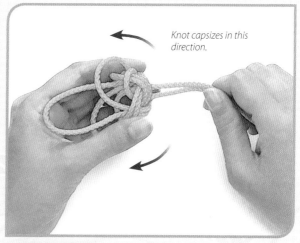

Knot capsizes in this direction.

As in Step 7 of the knife lanyard knot (p. 120), slide the knot off the hand. Capsize it into a 3-dimensional form by holding it in the left hand and pulling the ends to the right.

After doubling, or tripling, lead each end through the center opening from underneath. Gently pull the slack of the ends out through the knot.

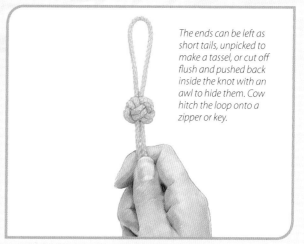

The ends can be left as short tails, unpicked to make a tassel, or cut off flush and pushed back inside the knot with an awl to hide them. Cow hitch the loop onto a zipper or key.

Work slack out of the knot, then tighten with an awl, working from the base of each side of the loop. Fair up into an even shape with a hammer, then re-tighten if necessary.

TOOL LANYARD

Tug one end and watch to see which bight moves. Pick up the bight with an awl to pull the end through the knot.

Tie the double knife lanyard knot (pp. 124–5), adjusting the loop to fit the neck or wrist. Find the last bight formed by either working end and pull it back through the knot.

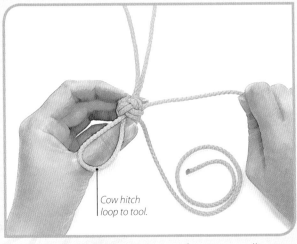

Cow hitch loop to tool.

Repeat Steps 8 and 9 three or four times, pulling out the first end and pulling the second end through the channel. This ensures that the loop will hold securely.

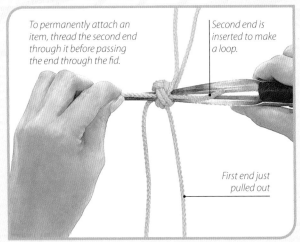

To permanently attach an item, thread the second end through it before passing the end through the fid.

Second end is inserted to make a loop.

First end just pulled out

Push a fid through the channel left by the working end just pulled out. Thread the second working end through the hollow of the fid. Pull it through the knot to create a loop.

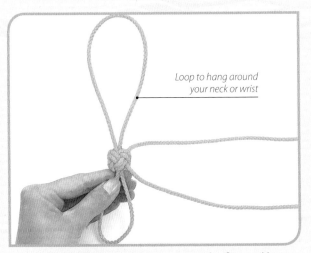

Loop to hang around your neck or wrist

For the final tuck, do not remove the first end but instead lead the second end alongside it. Make sure the knot is once again tight, then cut the ends off flush.

DECORATIVE

TURK'S HEAD (4-LEAD, 3-BIGHT)
•TURK'S HEAD (4-LEAD, 3-BIGHT): ALTERNATE

Turk's heads are a family of knots with one famous member, the Scout "woggle." They have long been associated with nautical ropework, both decorative and practical. Even today, the practice of tying one to mark the king spoke of a ship's wheel continues. Turk's heads are described by the number of leads, or interwoven strands forming the knot, and the number of bights, or curved edges along each rim.

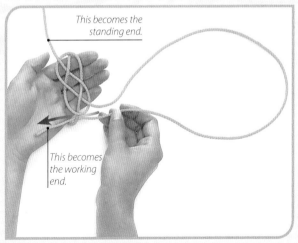

This becomes the standing end.

This becomes the working end.

Begin with Steps 1–4 of the knife lanyard knot (pp. 118–19). Lead the right, or lower, working end through the loop at the back of the hand, pull it through and let it hang.

DECORATIVE

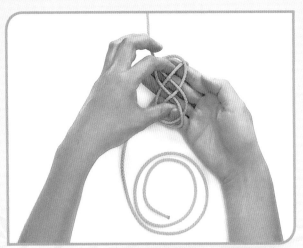

Slide the knot onto the fingers of the right hand. Poke the left index finger and thumb into the spaces above and below the center opening and pinch together.

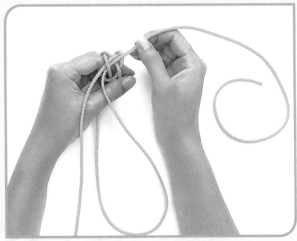

Slide the knot onto the index finger. Lead the working end into the knot parallel to, and below, the standing end. The knot is now locked and ready for doubling.

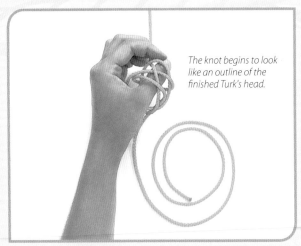

The knot begins to look like an outline of the finished Turk's head.

Slide the knot from the right hand, leaving it around the left thumb. Keep the knot very loose, but adjust the slack so that the knot is even and symmetrical.

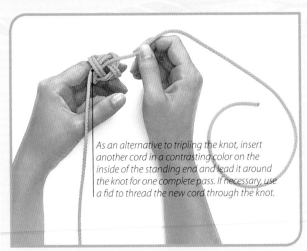

As an alternative to tripling the knot, insert another cord in a contrasting color on the inside of the standing end and lead it around the knot for one complete pass. If necessary, use a fid to thread the new cord through the knot.

Follow the knot until the working end reaches the beginning once more. The knot is now doubled.

DECORATIVE

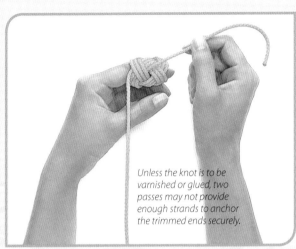

Unless the knot is to be varnished or glued, two passes may not provide enough strands to anchor the trimmed ends securely.

Follow the knot again once or twice and slide it onto the item to be decorated. Work out the slack with an awl. Cut the ends off close and push them under the standing parts.

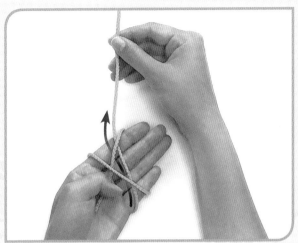

Lead the working end under both standing parts at the front of the hand to the right of where they cross.

TURK'S HEAD (4-LEAD, 3-BIGHT): ALTERNATE

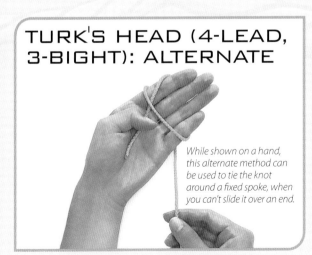

While shown on a hand, this alternate method can be used to tie the knot around a fixed spoke, when you can't slide it over an end.

Anchor the standing end with the thumb. Lead the working end to create two crossed standing parts at the front and two parallel standing parts at the back.

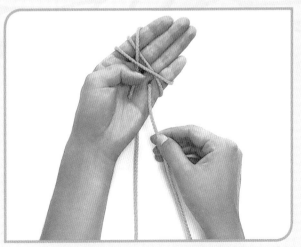

Now lead it behind the hand, across the left-hand standing part at the back, and to the front, left of all standing parts.

DECORATIVE

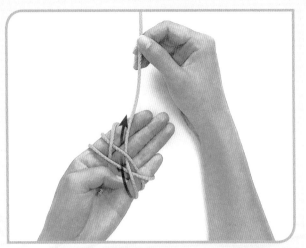

Bring it up over the first standing part and under the second, then turn the hand over.

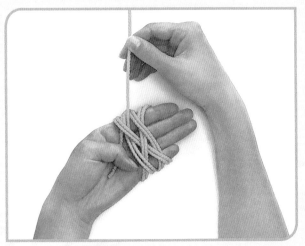

Lead the working end parallel to the standing end to lock the knot, then double it.

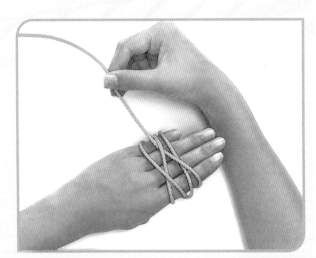

Take the working end over the first standing part, under the upper right of the crossed standing parts and then over the upper left. Turn the hand over.

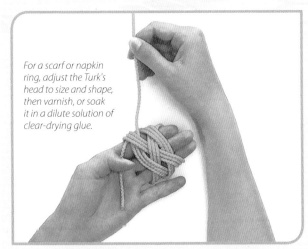

For a scarf or napkin ring, adjust the Turk's head to size and shape, then varnish, or soak it in a dilute solution of clear-drying glue.

As for Steps 5 and 6, follow the knot around as many times as required. Trim and conceal the ends.

TURK'S HEAD (3-LEAD, 5-BIGHT)

The three-lead, five-bight Turk's head produces a narrower band than its four-lead, three-bight cousin when tied in the same cord for the same number of passes. It is a circular version of the three-stranded plait used for long hair and for decorating horses' manes and tails. Turk's heads tied around the fingers can be slid over the end of an object before tightening but the same method is used to tie the knot directly around an object such as a fixed railing.

Lead the working end over the bottom right standing part and under the top right standing part.

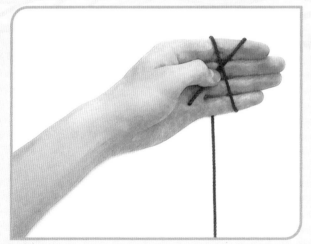

Anchor the standing end with the thumb. Lead the working end to create two crossed standing parts at the front and two parallel standing parts at the back.

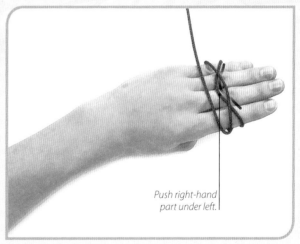

Push right-hand part under left.

Turn your hand over. Lead the working end to the left. Push the center of the right-hand standing part under the left to create two crossing points with a center opening.

DECORATIVE

Lead the working end up through the center opening from underneath. Now lead the working end under the standing part at the top right.

For a scarf or napkin ring, adjust the Turk's head to size and shape, then varnish, or soak it in a dilute solution of clear-drying glue.

Ease all the crossing points around the knot with an index finger until they are equally spaced. Follow the knot for as many passes as needed to make it the required width.

Turn the palm of the hand to face you once more. Lead the working end parallel to the standing part to lock the knot.

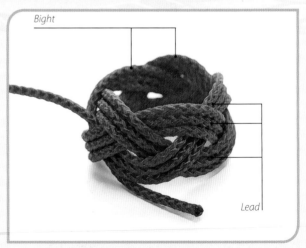

Bight

Lead

Work out the slack with an awl in several passes, cut the ends off close to where they emerge from the knot and push them underneath the standing parts.

SOLOMON BAR

Also called Portuguese sennit, Solomon bar is best known as a macramé knot used to make pot-plant hangers. Solomon bar zipper pulls and key fobs have a flat rather than spherical profile, and the same pattern can be used to make sturdy boat fenders in very thick rope. Combined with other knots, it makes an attractive, washable, and waterproof bracelet, or a hat band that can be pulled apart if necessary to provide extra cordage when camping. Solomon bar is wide enough to make a comfortable carry handle that won't cut into your hands.

Take the top end in front of, then behind, the right end, behind the bight, and up through the center of the loop formed in Step 1.

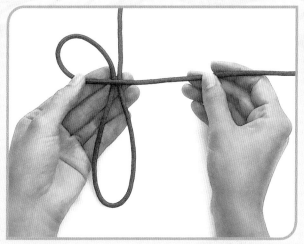

Middle a length of cord and, with the bight facing toward you, form a loop with the left-hand end by leading it in front of the bight and to the right.

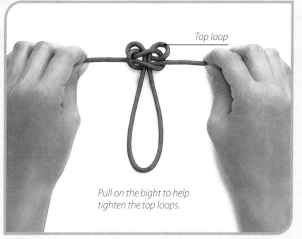

Top loop

Pull on the bight to help tighten the top loops.

Now reverse the tying process: lead the end now at right across the front, and the end at left in front of, then behind it, behind the bight, and up through the loop.

DECORATIVE

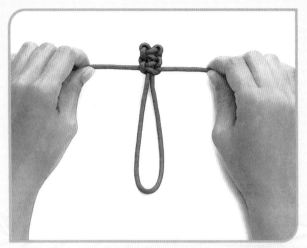

Continue knotting by taking the end that goes across the front of the work from the opposite side each time. If you take the end from the same side, the bar forms a spiral shape.

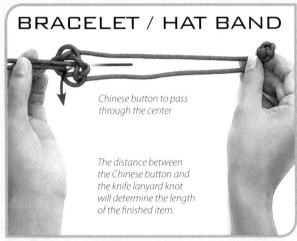

BRACELET / HAT BAND

Chinese button to pass through the center

The distance between the Chinese button and the knife lanyard knot will determine the length of the finished item.

Middle some cord and tie a Chinese button (p. 120). Tie a knife lanyard knot (pp. 118–20), with the Chinese button section forming the loop around the back of the hand.

Heat-sealed or glued end

When the piece is long enough, cut off each working end close to the knot and heat-seal or glue it in place. Cow hitch the loop onto a zipper or key, or attach a split ring.

The double loop will fasten over the button.

Push the Chinese button through the center of the knife lanyard knot. Tighten the knife lanyard knot around all four strands, after adjusting the length of the double loop.

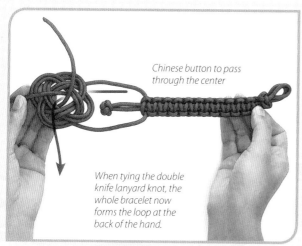

Chinese button to pass through the center

When tying the double knife lanyard knot, the whole bracelet now forms the loop at the back of the hand.

Begin the Solomon bar with the two long working ends. Continue to within 1 inch (2.5 cm) of the button. Tie a double knife lanyard knot (pp. 124–5).

HANDLE

Make sure this cord is the length needed for the finished handle.

To fit a carry handle, middle some cord, cow hitch it to one side of the item, and loop it through the other side. Make sure it is long enough to grasp comfortably.

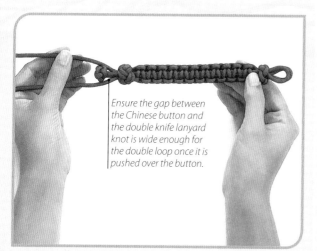

Ensure the gap between the Chinese button and the double knife lanyard knot is wide enough for the double loop once it is pushed over the button.

Push the Chinese button through the center of the double knife lanyard knot, and tighten the knot close to the end of the Solomon bar pattern. Cut working ends off flush.

Begin the Solomon bar pattern with the working ends and when the strap is finished, cut off and heat-seal or glue the ends as in Step 5.

DECORATIVE

ROPE LADDER

This portable, collapsible rope ladder is quick and simple to make, cannot rust, and is gentle on boat topsides and bare, wet feet. The ladder can be pulled apart easily and stowed as a rope coil when not in use or when the rope is needed for other purposes. It is light enough for children to carry, and to raise and lower. Because the rungs are not rigid, the ladder should be made only a little wider than a human foot. Space the rungs so that the distance from one to the next is comfortable for the smallest person who will use the ladder.

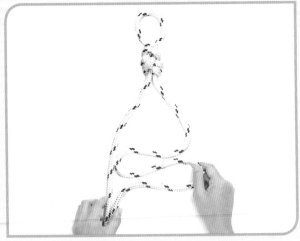

Tie a figure-of-eight loop (p. 34) in the middle of the rope. Make two bights in the right leg, forming a flat S-shape. The width of the S determines the width of the finished rung.

Pass the left leg from front to back through the eye of the upper bight and under both parts of the lower bight.

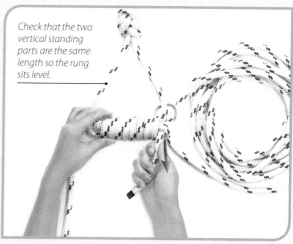

Check that the two vertical standing parts are the same length so the rung sits level.

Wind to the right until only the eye in the lower bight is exposed. Lead the leg over the rung to the back, around the right standing part, then feed it down through the eye.

Pass this leg away from you over the top of the bights, then bring it behind the bights to the front. Continue winding it tightly around the bights to form the first rung.

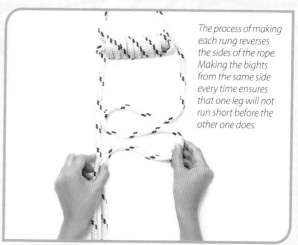

The process of making each rung reverses the sides of the rope. Making the bights from the same side every time ensures that one leg will not run short before the other one does.

The second rung is made the same way: by forming an S in the right leg, passing the left leg through the top bight and under the second, then winding from left to right.

GLOSSARY

ARBOR *The central part of a spool or reel about which line or cordage is wound.*

AWL *Thin metal spike with a handle, used to make holes in leather and canvas for sewing, for prising cordage out of knots where fingers can't reach and for pulling knots up snug.*

BEND *(noun) A knot joining the end of one rope to the end of another; (verb) To attach a rope to a spar or object, to attach a sail to a spar by means of a rope, to tie two ropes together at their ends.*

BIGHT *Any part of the cordage in between the two ends. Also, a section of rope bent back on itself in a flattened loop, ready for working into a knot.*

BINDING *Knot in a single piece of cordage that closes a bag opening, or confines, constricts, or lightly secures objects or coiled rope strands together.*

BLOCK *Enclosed device containing a sheave through which a rope passes in order to change its direction; a more nautical term for a pulley.*

BRAID LINE *Marine term for braided rope.*

BRAIDED ROPE *Cordage with interwoven strands proceeding both left and right, usually composed of one or more layers around an inner core.*

CAPSIZE *Distort a knot's layout, either accidentally by mishandling or overloading, or intentionally when tightening or working up a knot.*

CARABINER *Device similar to a snap hook but having features that make it particularly suited to climbing: it has a gate to prevent accidental release, and provision for rope to be belayed around it so as to be used as a brake.*

CLEW RING *The eyelet or cringle for attaching a sheet (controlling rope) to a sail.*

COIL *(noun) Rope neatly arranged so that it can be conveniently stored and transported; (verb) To arrange rope in a uniform shape so that it is manageable and doesn't tangle.*

CORDAGE *General term for any rope, line, or thin cord.*

CORE *The inner portion of a braided rope, usually the strongest part of the rope.*

CRINGLE *Metal sleeve, circular in shape, which can be sewn into a sail, or around which rope can be spliced. Its use is similar to that of a thimble.*

DOUBLE *To lead cordage, whether a new piece or a knot's own working end, exactly parallel to another to double the knot's bulk or width.*

EYE *Smallish circular formation in a hook, object, or rope, usually just large enough to allow the cordage, or bight of the cordage, to pass through.*

FAIR UP *Work or adjust a knot, usually decorative work, before and after the final tightening pass, so that it is evenly tensioned with a symmetrical or balanced appearance; may be done by lightly tapping all around with a hammer.*

FIBER *The basic material that the rope is made of—polyester, hemp, etc—or an individual strand of that material.*

FID *Spike or longish conical channel that is used to prize apart and open the lay of rope, wire, or knotting, so that another strand or piece of cordage can be fed through.*

FOLLOW *The process of leading a piece of cordage parallel to another.*

FRAPPING TURN *Non-structural lashing, applied more or less at right angles to an existing lashing, to compress or deflect it and increase its tension.*

GAFF *Spar, usually affixed to the upper, or upper forward, edge of a sail.*

HALF HITCH *The knot formed by making an underhand turn around an object, then leading the working end over the standing part.*

HALYARD *The cordage used to hoist a spar, sail, or flag.*

HEAVING LINE *Piece of light cordage with a bulky knot or small object attached to one end for throwing to another person or vessel.*

HITCH *(noun) A knot connecting a load-bearing rope to an object; (verb) To tie a half hitch or a succession of half hitches.*

JURY MAST *An emergency replacement mast, rigged around either a broken mast or another spar.*

LASHING *(noun) A knot, or succession of windings, that secures two or more structural items; (verb) The process of completing the knot or windings.*

LAID ROPE *Rope, traditional in appearance, that usually has three diagonally wound elements.*

LANYARD *Cordage, often decorative, that restrains an object, keeps it at the ready, or prevents it from being lost.*

LAY *The strands of the rope and the way that they twist. Hard and soft lay describes whether the strands are tightly or loosely wound.*

LOCKED *The state of a knot once the locking tuck is made.*

LOCKING TUCK *The final tuck with the working end that completes the knot structure.*

LOOP *Fixed or adjustable eye in a rope that can be attached to, or placed over, something; a knot that creates single or multiple, fixed or adjustable, loops.*

MARLINSPIKE *Metal or hardwood spike used to untie difficult knots, open the lay of rope or wire, and assist knotting procedures.*

MESSENGER/MOUSE *Line used to guide or pull a heavier rope into place.*

MIDDLE *To locate the center point of a length of rope.*

MONOFILAMENT *Single strand extruded filament.*

MULTIFILAMENT *Cordage made from fine strands of spun, wound, or plaited material.*

ON THE BIGHT *Term for a knot tied along a length of rope at a point other than its end.*

OVERHAND CROSSING *Similar to an overhand turn but the loop formed is not a perfect circle.*

OVERHAND TURN *Circle made by passing the working end over the standing part.*

PASS *The process of working once through a knot's complete structure, either leading the working end through to double the knot, or working a small amount of slack right through the knot and into the standing end.*

PASSING TURN *Pear or circular shape, formed almost accidentally by an independent process during the tying procedure.*

PENNANT STAFF *The rod or stick to which a small flag is attached when it is to be hoisted clear of the top of a mast and its rigging.*

PLAITED ROPE *Cordage with interwoven strands proceeding either diagonally left and right, or in the longitudinal direction of the rope.*

REEF POINT *A length of line attached to a sail for the purpose of gathering it in to reduce the sail area in a strong wind, or an eyelet to accept such a line.*

ROPE *Cordage of a thickness that can be comfortably worked or used in the hand.*

ROUND TURN *The formation made when a rope passes around an object one-and-a-half times.*

S-LAID *Less common form of laid rope, where the diagonal direction of the lay is left-handed.*

SENNIT *An item or length of cordage made by plaiting, braiding, or knotting.*

SHACKLE *U- or bow-shaped metal fastening device with a screw pin for closing and locking it.*

SHACKLE KEY *Slotted metal tool used to tighten and undo the screw pins of shackles; a shackle key and marlinspike are often combined in one tool.*

SHATTERED FILM ROPE *Rope made from flat, sheet-like strands rather than round fibers; relatively inexpensive and often made from residual material.*

SHEAVE *Wheel-like device over which rope runs in a block or pulley.*

SHEET *The cordage that performs the task of trimming a sail at its aft edge.*

SHOCK CORD *Elastic cordage, usually with a thin braided outer, with strands of rubber as an inner core.*

SIDE CUTTER *Tool for cutting light, single-stranded wire and nails, but also excellent for severing small cordage.*

SLING *An arrangement of a length of cordage that lifts and supports an object at the same time.*

SLIPPED KNOT *Knot tied with a bight made in the working end and used to make the final tuck. The knot can be released quickly by pulling the working end.*

SNAP HOOK *Hook with gate-type device that is quick to attach and has a spring loaded catch or pin for either quick release or to prevent it coming undone.*

SNUG *Pulled or worked until firmly up against something, or until all slack is removed.*

SPAR *This can refer to practically any pole on a vessel used for setting sail or supported by rigging; does not normally refer to the mast.*

SPLICING *The process of weaving or otherwise locking some, or all, of the strands of one rope to another.*

STANDING PART *The portion of rope leading up to, and into, the commencement of a knot; usually the part that is loaded.*

STOPPER *Knot preventing cordage from running through a hole or confined space.*

TACKLE *Blocks or pulleys, arranged to make a load easier to handle.*

TAIL *The leftover working end, once a knot is completed.*

THIMBLE *Metal or plastic sleeve, usually pear shaped, around which rope is spliced; its purpose is to prevent chafe and stop rope from closing tight around its fastening point.*

THIN CORD *Small-diameter cordage— also known as "small stuff"—too thin for practical handling under load but useful for decorative work, lanyards, and light-duty tasks.*

TOGGLE *Simple metal or wooden object, sometimes tailored for the purpose, that separates or secures portions of a knot, or joins the bights in separate lengths of rope.*

TUCK *(noun) The result after one strand has been fed under another; (verb) the process whereby one strand is fed under another.*

TURN *(noun) Cordage led over a spar, object, or another piece of rope, either simply draped over in u-shape, or fully passed around through 360 degrees; (verb) Leading cordage around a spar, object, or another piece of rope.*

UNDERHAND CROSSING *Similar to an underhand turn but the loop formed is not a perfect circle.*

UNDERHAND TURN *Circle made by passing the working end under the standing part.*

WHIPPING *The process in which rope, or its individual strands, is bound to prevent fraying, or when rope is bound to itself to form an eye.*

WHIPPING TWINE *Fine cordage used for whipping or heavy duty sewing.*

WORKING PART *The portion of the rope that is actively tying the knot; may be a bight.*

WORKING END *The end of the rope that is actively tying the knot but is not yet part of the knot; when the knot is completed, the tail or portion left over.*

Z-LAID *The common form of laid rope, where the diagonal direction of the lay is right-handed.*

			☆	▰	◤	⛰	🐟	⛵	🪝	WHAT'S IT FOR?
44	Alpine butterfly knot	2	✓	✓	✓	✓	✓	✓	✓	Attach flag clips, carabiners, and sinkers; simple ladder
76	Anchor bend	1		✓	✓			✓	✓	Attach anchor; secure tent stays; lift manhole cover
42	Angler's loop	2	✓				✓	✓	✓	Attach swivel to line; tether dinghy; loop in shock cord
48	Arbor knot	2	✓				✓			Attach rope to a drum, or fishing line to a reel; sliding loop
60	Ashley's bend	2	✓	✓				✓		Join different ropes; join fine lines; four-way tie-down
26	Bag knot	1	✓	✓					✓	Secure the top of a bag or sack or a rolled mat or bundle
75	Barrel hitch	1	✓						✓	Hoist a barrel, statue, or square-based box
46	Blood loop dropper knot	2					✓			Attach branch line to main fishing line
30	Bottle sling	3	✓	✓	✓				✓	Lift or carry a bottle, flask, or canister
36	Bowline	2	✓	✓	✓	✓	✓	✓	✓	Practical knot; attach rope to a pole; join dissimilar rope
40	Bowline on the bight	2	✓				✓	✓	✓	Form twin loops in fishing line; irregularly shaped objects
79	Buntline hitch	2						✓	✓	Attach sheets to a sail, clew ring, or snap shackle
59	Carrick bend	1	✓					✓	✓	Join heavy ropes
72	Clove hitch	1	✓	✓			✓	✓	✓	Attach rope to a pole; make a temporary barrier fence
28	Constrictor knot	1	✓	✓			✓	✓	✓	Tie bundles of pliable material; secure strands of a laid rope
68	Cow hitch	1	✓	✓			✓	✓	✓	Attach a ring to a closed loop, or a lanyard to a camera
95	Diagonal lashing	2	✓	✓					✓	Scouting activities; secure poles at odd angles
121	Double Chinese button	3	✓							Bulkier soft button or frog-style fastener
124	Double knife lanyard knot	3	✓				✓			Bulkier zipper pull or key fob; lanyard for small objects
102	Eye splice	2	✓					✓	✓	Make an eye in the end or join two pieces of laid rope
55	Figure-of-eight bend	1	✓	✓	✓			✓	✓	Join ropes of the same diameter; add length to stays
19	Figure-of-eight knot	1	✓	✓	✓	✓		✓	✓	Stop rope from running through a hole; a decorative knot
34	Figure-of-eight loop	1	✓	✓	✓	✓	✓	✓	✓	Attach item to a rope; make a fixed loop; hang an object
56	Fisherman's knot	2	✓	✓	✓	✓	✓	✓	✓	Join line, rope or cord; adjustable fastenings for necklaces
108	Handcuffs puzzle	1	✓							Escape from interlocked rope handcuffs
80	Highwayman's hitch	2	✓					✓	✓	Secure a dinghy temporarily
107	Impossible knot	1	✓							Tie a knot without letting go of either end of the rope
52	Jury mast knot	3			✓			✓	✓	Rig a jury mast, tent post, or flagpole; decorative trim
118	Knife lanyard knot	3	✓							Simple zipper pull or key fob; soft button or fastener
114	Kringle mat	2	✓				✓			Functional or decorative floor or table mat; drink coaster
74	Marlinspike hitch	2	✓				✓	✓	✓	Provide good grip on thin cord; hoist a tool by the handle

#	Knot	★	▱	◩	⛰	🍃	⌁	⌐	WHAT'S IT FOR?
112	Monkey's fist	3	✓	✓			✓	✓	Heaving line; key float and fob; zipper pull; dog toy
110	Not a knot	1	✓						Make a reef knot disappear without untying it
116	Ocean mat	2	✓				✓		Easy-to-tie functional or decorative oval mat; doormat
64	One-way sheet bend	2	✓	✓	✓	✓	✓		Pull a large rope along a dock; hoist a rope up a cliff
17	Overhand knot	1	✓	✓	✓	✓	✓	✓	Prevent rope from slipping through a hole
86	Palomar knot	1	✓			✓			Attach hooks or other items to fishing line
70	Pile hitch	1	✓				✓	✓	Tether a dinghy to a pile or bollard; tie between posts
24	Pole lashing	1	✓	✓				✓	Tie a bundle of poles; suspend a plank
78	Prusik knot	1	✓	✓	✓		✓	✓	Climbing rope handhold or equipment attachment
22	Reef knot	1	✓	✓			✓	✓	Tie reef points in sails; tie parcels; flat knot in cloth
65	Rigger's bend	2	✓	✓	✓		✓		Join ropes of similar size and texture; join slippery ropes
109	Ring drop	1	✓						Remove a ring threaded on a loop without letting go
83	Rolling hitch	2	✓	✓			✓	✓	Fasten rope to take load at an angle
136	Rope ladder	2	✓	✓			✓		A soft, collapsible, light-weight, transportable ladder
97	Sheer lashing	1	✓	✓				✓	Reinforce or extend a pole; create an A-frame
62	Sheet bend	1	✓	✓			✓	✓	Join ropes of equal or different size
104	Short splice	3	✓				✓	✓	Permanently join two lengths of laid rope
88	Snelling a hook	2				✓			Attach fishing line to a hook
133	Solomon bar	2	✓	✓			✓		Flat zipper pull or key fob; bracelet or hat band; carry handle
50	Spanish bowline	2	✓					✓	Hoist and suspend irregularly shaped objects
93	Square lashing	1	✓	✓				✓	Scouting activities; build light framework or garden trellis
58	Surgeon's knot: bend	1	✓	✓		✓		✓	Join cotton and thread; join fishing line
21	Surgeon's knot: binding	1	✓	✓		✓			Leatherwork; any tying-off using fine line, twine, or thin cord
35	Surgeon's loop	1	✓			✓		✓	Permanent loops in the end of shock cord or fishing line
82	Timber hitch	1	✓	✓				✓	Lift and haul a log; attach nylon guitar strings to the bridge
85	Topsail halyard bend	2	✓			✓			Hoist a pennant staff or topsail spar; lift a pole
32	Transom knot	1	✓	✓				✓	Temporary lashing; craft; gardening trellises; kite frames
99	Tripod lashing	2	✓	✓				✓	Support for suspending bell or pot; frame for teepee
90	Trucker's hitch	2	✓	✓				✓	Tie a load to a trailer; tension tent stays
131	Turk's head (3-lead, 5-bight)	3	✓				✓		Tubular knot; grip or trim on handle; napkin or scarf ring
127	Turk's head (4-lead, 3-bight)	3	✓				✓	✓	Tubular knot; grip or trim on handle; napkin or scarf ring

HOW DO I?

Keep rope from tangling in the car boot or a rope locker	Wrapped coil, bundled coil
Hang hanks of rope for storage	Bundled coil, double slip coil
Tie tent ropes so they can be tensioned	Trucker's hitch
Tie down a load on a trailer, secure a cover over it	Trucker's hitch
Tie a tool to a rope for hoisting aloft	Marlinspike hitch, bowline on the bight/Spanish bowline
Tie a rope to the handle of a bucket or paint tin for hoisting	Round turn and two half hitches on the handle
Hoist a paint tin with no handle	Barrel hitch
Make a zipper easier to grab hold of	Solomon bar, knife lanyard knot, or a monkey's fist
Stop the end of a rope from fraying	Common, French, or West country whipping
Hang items with a knot that can be untied from the ground	Highwayman's hitch
Join pieces of shock cord; tie a loop in shock cord	Ashley's and rigger's bends; angler's loop
Tie planks or branches together for carrying or lifting	Pole lashing
Put a new carry handle on a case	Solomon bar
Join two ropes with a knot that won't catch when hauled	One-way sheet bend
Make a transportable lightweight ladder	Rope ladder knot
Tie a load onto roof racks	Rolling hitch, anchor bend, round turn and two half hitches
Weight the end of a line for throwing	Monkey's fist
Stop the end of a rope passing through a block	Figure-of-eight knot
Tie a fish hook in fishing line	Palomar knot, snelling a hook
Get a good grip on small or slippery line to pull hard	Marlinspike hitch
Put a loop in a rope when the ends are not accessible	Alpine butterfly knot, figure-of-eight loop; bowline on the bight or Spanish bowline
Suspend a plank as a temporary shelf	Pole lashings finished with bowlines; alternate bowline for attaching to support points
Suspend a pot over a campfire	Tripod lashing
Decorate a walking stick, a ship's wheel or tiller handle	Turk's head
Improve grip on varnished or slippery wheels or tool handles	Turk's head, French whipping in cord rather than twine
Attach a closed loop to a ring or other closed eye fitting	Cow hitch
Rig up a temporary clothesline in a tent or between tents	Tautline hitch
Make a temporary swing with an old tire	Bowline with standing part threaded through loop around the support; alternate bowline around tire
Fit a cable tie to an electrical lead for securing the coiled lead	Constrictor knot midway on lead with ends long enough to tie a reef knot round the coiled lead
Stop a dressing gown cord from fraying	Overhand knot, figure-of-eight knot
Secure a bead to cord to make a lamp switch pull	Overhand knot, figure-of-eight knot; monkey's fist
Make a doormat from old rope; make drink coasters	Ocean mat; kringle mat
Hang items from vertical tent poles or rope	Prusik knot
Make frames and trellis for the garden	Transom knot; square and diagonal lashing
Stop small tools being dropped or lost	Tool lanyard made from double knife lanyard knot
Stop keys dropped in the water from sinking	Monkey's fist key fob with buoyant core

INDEX

alpine butterfly knot 44–5
alternate bowline 36, 39
alternate clove hitch 72, 73
alternate Turk's head, 4-lead,
3-bight 129–30
anchor bend 54, 67, 76–7
angler's knot 56
angler's loop 42–3
arbor knot 48–9
Ashley's bend 60–1

bag knot 26–7
barrel hitch 75
bends 54
bight 7
bindings 20
blood knot 57
blood loop dropper knot 46–7
bottle sling 30–1
bowline on the bight 40–1
bowlines 36–41, 50–1
braided rope 7, 8
bundled coil 15
buntline hitch 79

carrick bend 59
Chinese button 120
clove hitches 6, 72–3, 85
common whipping 12
constrictor knot 28–9
cordage 6
   types 8–9
cow hitch 68
cow hitch and toggle 69

decorative knots 111
diagonal lashing 95–6
dolly knot 90–1
double bowline 36, 37–8
double Chinese button 121–3
double fisherman's knot 57

double knife lanyard knot
124–5
double pile hitch 70, 71
double sheet bend 62, 63
double slip coil 15

eye splice 101, 102–3

figure-of-eight bend 55
figure-of-eight knot 16, 19
figure-of-eight loop 34
fisherman's bend
   see anchor bend
fisherman's knot 56
Flemish bend 55
French whipping 13

granny knot 23

half hitch 6
handcuffs puzzle 108
highwayman's hitch 80–1
hitches 67
hooks, snelling 88–9
Hunter's bend 65–6

impossible knot 107

jug sling 30–1
jury mast knot 52–3

killick hitch 82
knife lanyard knot 118–20
kringle mat 114–15

laid rope 7, 8
lanyards 111, 118–20, 124–6
lashings 20, 92
ligature knot 58
loops 33

marlinspike hitch 74
mats 111, 114–17
monkey's fist 112–13
multiple overhand 16, 17–18

not a knot 110

ocean mat 116–17
Oklahoma hitch 24–5
one-way sheet bend 64
overhand knots 17–18
overhand turn 7

palomar knot 86–7
pedigree cow hitch 68, 69
pile hitch 70–1
plank sling 25
pole lashing 24–5
Portuguese sennit 133–5
Prusik knot 78

reef knot 22–3
rigger's bend 65–6
ring drop 109
rolling hitch 83–4, 85
rope
   coiling 14–15
   cutting 11
   sealing 11
rope care 8
rope ladder 136–7
rope tricks 106
round turn 6
round turn and two half
hitches 77
running loops 33

scaffold hitch 24–5
sheer lashing 97–8
sheet bend 62–3
short splice 101, 104–5

S-laid rope 7
slipped bag knot 26, 27
slipped constrictor knot 29
slipped overhand 17, 18
snelling 88–9
Solomon bar 111, 133–5
Spanish bowline 50–1
splices 101
square lashing 93–4
standing end 7
stopper knots 16
surgeon's knot bend 58
surgeon's knot binding 21
surgeon's loop 35

tautline hitch 83, 84
timber hitch 82
tool lanyard 126
tools 10
topsail halyard bend 67, 85
transom knot 32
tripod lashing 99–100
trucker's hitch 90–1
tucked sheet bend 64
Turk's head 111
   3-lead, 5-bight 131–2
   4-lead, 3-bight 127–30
turns 6

underhand turn 7

waggoner's hitch 90–1
water bowline 36, 38
West country whipping 13
whipping 12–13
working end 7
wrapped coil 14

Z-laid rope 7

ACKNOWLEDGMENTS

The publishers wish to thank Bob Doel, David Glasson, Colin Grundy, Geoff Magee, Gordon Perry, the Rushcutter Shipchandlers, Geoff Smithson, Angie Turnbull, and Jonny Wells for their assistance in the production of this volume.

About the authors

Neville Olliffe and **Madeleine Rowles-Olliffe**, both members of the International Guild of Knot Tyers (IGKT), have run a small business making and selling handmade items of knotting and rope work for almost 20 years.

Neville began sailing as a teenager and, in 1968, took on a job in the marine trade and began a part-time writing career. He and Madeleine own one of Sydney's oldest yachts, which keeps them up to date with whipping and splices. Neville's focus is on basic knots and their usage, and various splicing techniques.

Madeleine, a systems engineer from an electronics and telecommunications background, is interested in applied and decorative knotting, and participated in IGKT public demonstrations at Hobart's biennial Australian Wooden Boat Festival in 2007 and 2009.

Disclaimer

While the material in this book has been prepared with your safety and the security of your property in mind, the authors and publishers accept no responsibility for the manner in which rope and knots are used. Be aware that a rope or knot that is suitable in one situation might be inappropriate in another, and caution must always be taken. Any suggested or implied usage is based on historical or common application, and ultimate responsibility lies with the common sense of the reader. Always proceed in a careful and cautious manner and seek qualified specialist advice from a professional before undertaking anything risky.

Neville Olliffe

Madeleine Rowles-Olliffe (left) seen here with Jasmine Parker, giving instructions on how to tie a knot.